PRAISE FOR *THE CALL*

"*The Call* provides a first-hand deep dive into the facts of how
Saudi Arabia spawned Salafi movements abroad that now are
largely self-sustaining, as the kingdom yields to global pressure (and the reality of diminished oil revenues) by curbing its
external spending to spread fundamentalist Islam. These days,
when so few journalists bother to dig for facts, preferring to
pontificate, Krithika Varagur's work stands out."

Karen Elliott House
Author of *On Saudi Arabia: Its People, Past,
Religion, Fault Lines—and Future* and winner of
the Pulitzer Prize for International Reporting

"A comprehensive analysis of Saudi Arabia's decades of proselytizing its ultraconservative Islamic views throughout the
world. Based on meticulous research and field work, this is
the best account in print of how our ally has spread its intolerance and extremism, but also how that has evolved over time.
A must-read for Islam watchers."

Bruce Riedel
Director of the Brookings Intelligence Project,
Brookings Institution, author of *Kings and Presidents:
Saudi Arabia and the United States Since FDR*

The Call
Inside the Global Saudi Religious Project

COLUMBIA GLOBAL REPORTS
NEW YORK

The Call
Inside the Global Saudi Religious Project

Krithika Varagur

Kosovo

Pristina

Peja

Kacanik

Saudi Arabia

Medina

Riyadh

Mecca

Jeddah

Nigeria

Kano

Maiduguri

Abuja

Atlantic Ocean

© 2020 Jeffrey L. Ward

Published with support from the Andrew W. Mellon Foundation

The Call
Inside the Global Saudi Religious Project
Copyright © 2020 by Krithika Varagur
All rights reserved

Published by Columbia Global Reports
91 Claremont Avenue, Suite 515
New York, NY 10027
globalreports.columbia.edu
facebook.com/columbiaglobalreports
@columbiaGR

Library of Congress Cataloging-in-Publication Data
Names: Varagur, Krithika, author.
Title: The Call : Inside the Global Saudi Religious Project / Krithika Varagur.
Description: New York, NY: Columbia Global Reports, 2020. | Includes
    bibliographical references. |
Identifiers: LCCN 2020006024 | ISBN 9781733623766 (paperback) | ISBN
    9781733623773 (ebook)
Subjects: LCSH: Wahhābīyah. | Salafīyah. | Islam and state--Saudi
    Arabia. | Islam--Saudi Arabia. | Islamic fundamentalism. | Saudi
    Arabia--Relations--Islamic countries. | Islamic
    countries--Relations--Saudi Arabia.
Classification: LCC BP195.W2 V37 2020 | DDC 297.8/1409--dc23
LC record available at https://lccn.loc.gov/2020006024

Book design by Strick&Williams
Map design by Jeffrey L. Ward
Author photograph by Miranda Sita

Printed in the United States of America

CONTENTS

GLOSSARY

alim/ulama: Muslim religious scholars (singular/plural)

bidah: heretical innovation in religious matters

dawa: literally "the call" or "invitation" to Islam, it refers to proselytization more generally

fiqh: human understanding of the divine Islamic law, which has several distinct traditions

hajj: the pilgrimage to Mecca required of all able-bodied Muslims in their lifetime

mujahideen: those engaged in jihad, especially guerrilla fighters fighting against non-Muslim forces

sharia: Islamic law derived from the Quran, *sunnah,* and traditions of jurisprudence

shirk: the sin of idolatry or polytheism and violating *tawhid* by worshipping anything other than God

sunnah: the actions and sayings traditionally ascribed to the Prophet Muhammad

tawhid: the doctrine of the oneness of God

Izala: The Society of Removal of Innovation and Re-establishment of the Sunna, a Salafi movement based in Northern Nigeria

Salafism: A revivalist Sunni Islamic movement to return to the traditions of the *salaf,* the first three generations of Muslims. It was founded in late nineteenth-century Egypt as a reaction to Western colonialism and imperialism.

Shia Islam: one of the two main branches of Islam, followed by about a tenth of Muslims, especially in Iran, that rejects the first three Sunni caliphs and regards Ali, the fourth caliph, as Muhammad's first true successor

Sufism: the mystical tradition in Islam that emphasizes direct personal experience of God and whose followers often organize into orders around a teacher who traces a direct chain of successive teachers back to the Prophet Muhammad

Sunni Islam: one of the two main branches of Islam, followed by about 90 percent of Muslims, that believes that the caliph Abu Bakr was the rightful successor to Muhammad after his death

Wahhabism: an ultraconservative religious movement founded by the eighteenth-century Arabian preacher Muhammad ibn Abd al-Wahhab that focuses on removing idolatry and innovations in Islam, which became the official religion of Saudi Arabia after Ibn Abd al-Wahhab signed a pact with the royal House of Saud

DDII: the Indonesian Islamic Dawa Council

FPI: the Islamic Defenders' Front, a hardline Indonesian Islamist group founded in 1998

IIRO: the International Islamic Relief Organization, a Saudi charity founded in 1978

IUM: the Islamic University of Medina, an international university that opened in 1962

LIPIA: the Islamic and Arabic College of Indonesia in Jakarta, which opened in 1980 as a branch of Riyadh's Imam Muhammad ibn Saud University

MWL: the Muslim World League, the most important *dawa*-oriented Saudi charity, founded in 1962 and headquartered in Mecca

WAMY: the World Assembly of Muslim Youth, a Saudi charity founded in Riyadh in 1972

Introduction

You had to admit the optics were good. Two hundred thousand people, all dressed in white, radiated from the Hotel Indonesia roundabout in Central Jakarta. In drone photographs the effect is serene: at the center is the socialist realist Welcome monument, punctuating a circular pool, and in the five broad roads branching off from it, like the avenues that radiate from the Arc d'Triomphe, protesters clog the streets for a mile in every direction. They went all the way up to the National Monument and beyond, to the Presidential Palace. They came on buses, planes, boats, and on foot from all across Java and even other islands to participate in the largest Islamist demonstration in Indonesian history. The date itself was memorable: November 4, 2016, or "411."

"We came to the Palace to enforce the law," said the cleric Habib Rizieq Shihab, to rapt silence. "Desecrators of the Quran must be punished. We must reject the leaders of infidels—it is forbidden to accept the leadership of infidels, and of people of the Chinese race," he said, exhorting the crowd to reject Ahok, the Chinese-Christian governor of Indonesia's capital city. "If

14 our demands are not heard, are you ready to turn this into a revolution?" "We're ready!" screamed the crowd, breaking into
huge applause. They added, spontaneously: "God is great!" And
others: "Kill Ahok!"

It was a bizarre scene in Indonesia, which is the world's
largest Muslim-majority country but is not really a "Muslim
nation." Officially, it is a multifaith country that protects six
religions equally, where race and ethnicity have been tacitly
elided from political discourse. An overtly Muslim political
protest like this had no precedent.

Shihab, who is an Indonesian of Yemeni descent, appeared
to the crowd like a small god, dressed in white robes and a jade-
green turban, unaffected by the heat. Not a drop of rain hit Jakarta
that day, which is unusual this close to the equator, and it seemed,
indeed, like a sign from God.

The 411 rally was billed as an *aksi damai,* a peaceful protest.
It may have been peaceful in format—it was fairly well organized
and staffed with thousands of volunteers—but it was virulently hateful in content. The Islamic Defenders Front (FPI),
led by Shihab, organized the protest as a show of force against
Basuki Tjahaja Purnama, widely known as "Ahok," the governor
of Jakarta. They accused him of blasphemy against Islam and
called for his ouster. The pretext was later revealed to be a bank-
rupt one, since the "evidence" for Ahok's crime was a doctored
video of him referencing a Quran verse. This was not really
about Ahok, however, but about displaying the piety and political power of Muslim Indonesians—and for that, it worked.
The city shut down all its major arteries that day. At the second
"peaceful protest," on December 12, the president of Indonesia
himself joined them in prayer.

The FPI's campaign was more successful than they could have dreamed: the Christian governor lost his bid for reelection, and on top of that, he was sentenced to two years in jail. This was a turning point for political Islam in Indonesia, which had never before pierced the public sphere to such an extent. The next presidential election was waged largely on the terms set by the events of 2016, and the vice president of Indonesia today was once its highest Muslim cleric. Both of the 2019 presidential candidates campaigned on their Islamic credentials, and both took whirlwind trips to Mecca just days before the election. Shihab's ahistorical vision came to look like a portent.

So where is Shihab today? He's not enjoying the fruits of his labor in Indonesia. He is actually in Saudi Arabia. After the gubernatorial election, he became embroiled in a sexting scandal and fled a warrant for his arrest to Mecca. It is actually not such an unusual choice of refuge, because Shihab's ties to the kingdom stretch rather far back. As a young man in the 1980s, he studied Arabic at the Islamic and Arabic College of Indonesia (LIPIA), a unique Indonesian university in South Jakarta built, funded, and fully subsidized to this day by Saudi Arabia. He went on to study for four years in Riyadh, where he networked with Saudi clerics and burnished his religious credentials. He came back to Indonesia when it became a democracy in 1998 and quickly consolidated his stature as a populist religious vigilante, raiding bars and brothels in Jakarta through his newly formed Islamic Defenders Front.

That his organization and vision became so powerful is just one example of how Saudi Arabia influenced many of the conservative religious figures who went on to shape modern Indonesia. Another infamous example is the Bali bombings of 2002,

16 which killed 202 people, mostly tourists, in the world's most deadly terror attack post-9/11. The attacks were planned by a circle of jihadists based at the Al-Mukmin Islamic boarding school in Central Java, which was founded with a gift from the Saudi king in 1972. A dense jihadi network coalesced around the school, which was the alma mater of four of the Bali bombers.

Beyond such flagship investments, more than fifty years of Saudi proselytizing in Indonesia also seeded the virulent intolerance of religious minorities that plagues the country today. In addition to the show trial of its most prominent Christian politician, Indonesia is also now a country where there is a national "Anti-Shia" league and where Ahmadiyya Muslims have been driven from their homes by mobs into refugee camps.

As the world's largest Muslim-majority nation and a developing, postcolonial state, Indonesia has been subject to the full spectrum of Saudi Arabia's ambitious campaign of proselytization. And while Saudi investments peaked at least a decade ago, as they have in most of the world, their legacy effects are copious. Today, there is a thriving ecosystem of ultraconservative Salafis not just in Indonesia but across Southeast Asia, from Thailand to the Philippines. Saudi investments have fueled jihadis, helped consolidate Indonesia's leading Islamist political party, and produced dozens of ideologues like Habib Riziq Shihab. The Saudi soft power apparatus in Indonesia is unrivaled and includes a dedicated university, large embassy, and powerful, stand-alone "religious attaché." Saudi charities also helped put thousands of students in a still-developing country into school and university and helped rebuild devastated regions, like Aceh, after the 2004 Boxing Day tsunami.

It's not for nothing that Barack Obama, who spent years in Jakarta, pointedly remarked on the "more fundamentalist, unforgiving interpretation" of Islam that he perceived when he returned there as an adult, which he attributed to Saudi influence. In doing so, he joined an already flourishing discourse of *Arabisasi*.

Arabisasi was one of the first Indonesian words I learned after I moved to Jakarta in 2016. It is a neologism meaning "Arabization" in Bahasa Indonesia (Indonesian) and it connotes a whole class of developments: the rise of political Islam, blasphemy charges, the growing popularity of hijabs and burqas, new mosques, louder mosques, new schools, the persecution of religious minorities, *sharia* bylaws, and an overall new, visible centrality of Islam in the cultural and political life of a big democracy that was, until 1998, a tightly controlled military dictatorship.

The underlying claim of Arabisasi is that five decades of Saudi Arabia's religious influence in Indonesia had in some way caused all these diverse phenomena. Regardless of how true or false this is, the word points to a generalized anxiety over "Saudi money," in Indonesia as in the rest of the world. It seemed to neatly explain how a tropical archipelago reputed for its tolerance and syncretism was, by the time I got there in 2016, a theater for hardline Islamists, begrudging at best and violent at worst toward religious minorities, and even the home of a few hundred foreign fighters to ISIS.

Saudi Arabia did not cause the conservative turn in Indonesia. But I learned, through a sustained inquiry, that it had indeed helped with quite a lot of its component parts, quite a

18   lot of the time. What surprised me was the scale, breadth, and personalized outreach behind the Saudi campaign in Indonesia, which started in the 1960s when a disgraced politician, sidelined by the secular new nation, found a sympathetic ear in Saudi Arabia's King Faisal, who was simultaneously prototyping his idea of a foreign policy driven by "Islamic solidarity." What impressed me further was the range of this campaign's effects: not merely superficial conservatism in dress and practice, but also strident campaigns against minority Muslim sects, the consolidation of a highly organized Islamist political party, and the influential alumni roster of a single, small Saudi-funded university.

I traveled through much of the Indonesian archipelago, from Aceh to Sulawesi, and was continually impressed by Saudi actors' broad vision of combining aid and proselytization, from tsunami relief in Banda Aceh to a homegrown Salafi group called Wahdah Islamiyah in Makassar. The line was always blurred.

This book began as a personal exploration and investigation of the country where I lived for two years and expanded in scope when I realized Saudi Arabia's export of its religion was a global project. The reason Salafis on six continents today read the same books is because they can, and a reason they can is that Saudi Arabia printed and shipped out those books around the world over the last half-century. So, I expanded my inquiry to two more places in the wider Muslim world: Nigeria and Kosovo. Three continents, three case studies. It could have been replicated with three different countries, several times over, and I hope it is. There is official Saudi *dawa*, or proselytization, activity in two dozen countries and unofficial Saudi proselytization in many more.

Saudi Arabia's global export of Wahhabism, sometimes dubbed "petro-Islam," because it dovetailed with its explosion of its oil wealth since 1973, has been an irresistible phenomenon to cite in the post-9/11 world, where religious conservatism is often collapsed into extremism and terrorism, and they are all jointly seen as a problem to be solved. But because "petro-Islam" is such a blunt rhetorical cudgel, the actual effects of Saudi proselytization are poorly understood and are rarely connected across specific contexts. For instance, it's not just "the Saudi government" that spreads Wahhabism; international Saudi actors include universities, an Islamic Affairs ministry, several state-adjacent global charities like the Muslim World League, one-off regional relief efforts, and independent businessmen.

This book is about the effects of Saudi proselytization in three peacetime, democratic Muslim-majority countries outside the Middle East: Indonesia, Nigeria, and Kosovo. From considering these countries together, some key themes emerge about what Saudi proselytization does abroad. It typically encourages Salafi communities, consisting of conservative Muslims who follow the revivalist movement to return to the traditions of early Islam. Saudi proselytization tends to cultivate a learned Salafi class of scholars and ideologues who then shape their local religious landscapes. It leads to the often-violent intolerance of Shia and Sufi Muslims, as well as minority sects like the Ahmadiyya and other faiths like Christianity. It is linked to a greater popular consumption of Salafi books, TV, radio, and online media. Saudi outreach is always multilateral. In its early years, it's usually also personal and depends on close, in-country contacts. And perhaps most important: as many of their effects are incidental as they are intentional. Even though

20 Wahhabism has a strict, literalist, fundamentalist approach to matters of theology, its expressions in Saudi foreign policy have been rather like—not to put too fine a point on it—throwing spaghetti against a wall to see what sticks. Still, in its ambition and global reach, the Saudi project has been unparalleled in the Muslim world.

Sometimes the communities that arise out of Saudi dawa provide a ready-made base for Salafi-jihadism, which has been their most notorious effect today. This was, in distinct ways, basically the case with Boko Haram in Nigeria and with ISIS foreign fighters in Kosovo. Especially in the pre-9/11 era, unchecked money flowed out from the kingdom, often from independent businessmen, supporting sundry terror groups from Somalia to Syria. But it's sometimes hard to draw a direct connection. For instance, a lot of Saudi support for people who would eventually become terrorists was wrapped up with the Soviet-Afghan war effort, which was also heavily supported by the US. It's hard to imagine that they knew the Indonesians who fought in the Afghan *mujahideen* would go on to conduct several high-profile bombings in Southeast Asia.

The Saudi project can be chaotic and full of contradictions, both supporting and rigidly denouncing Muslim Brotherhood activists, or simultaneously funding shady charities and counterextremism centers that work within miles of each other. It's not so unlike America's international exploits during the Cold War, which took forms both serious (coups) and unserious (the *Paris Review*), and was decentralized across various actors (the CIA, State Department, the Army, NASA) in service of a vague goal.

Not to mention that the country doing all this exporting is one of the world's strangest societies: an extremely religious, absolute, hereditary monarchy with thousands of royals, no set line of succession, and a state apparatus built from scratch in the last hundred years. It is a kingdom with a looming class of fearful Wahhabi clerics whose power waxes and wanes unpredictably, but whose support is essential to the ruling dynasty.

The Call is a window into a world changed by that kingdom and its oil money. It's the story of how one nation has tried to systematically transform the Muslim world, and Muslims in the world, in its image. Since the middle of the previous century, Saudi Arabia has spent billions of dollars to propagate its puritanical brand of Islam abroad to chaotic but also patterned effect.

Since 9/11, two aspects of Saudi dawa have been most studied: terror finance and textbooks. The terrorism concern is valid but limited, because in any country, terrorists are a tiny minority. And textbooks are a concrete subject of study, which is why American officials have periodically targeted them, but in the grand scheme of dawa materials, they are only a small component. We rarely talk about the other massive effects of Saudi dawa in terms of intolerance, fundamentalism, and Salafi leaders, which can reshape the cultural landscape of huge countries from within and create great religious and cultural strife. In Nigeria and Indonesia, both Saudi alumni and Saudi-influenced Salafis have taken powerful roles in government, whereas in Kosovo, religious leaders stand mostly at odds with an insistently secular government but command huge grassroots audiences.

Finally, we must not overstate what Saudi money has done or can do. When you talk about such a huge, multi-armed

22 project, it never works out the way you think it will, and especially not today, when its spending power is much diminished. Much of the discourse on Saudi proselytization seems like it ossified ten or twenty years in the past and rarely takes in the whole project in its full geographical scope. This book is a corrective to that and to the reflexive ascription of any conservative religious trend, from more women wearing hijabs to louder mosques to "Saudi influence."

Understanding the Saudi dawa project is crucial to understanding the 20th century. The project is entangled with the Cold War, the Third World, and fundamentalisms. As it slowly spun out from a personal project of the highest Saudi monarchs into a diffuse effort with thousands of funders and beneficiaries, it became harder and harder to control and predict, encompassing everything from terrorist incubation to disaster relief. But all of this must be part of what we talk about when we talk about Saudi money.

The Call

Islam started in Saudi Arabia in 622 and oil was discovered in Saudi Arabia in 1938. Between those landmark events, it was not a world power. Parts of what is now the theocratic nation-state of Saudi Arabia belonged to some of the great Islamic empires—Umayyad, Abbasid, Ottoman—and others to a shifting catalog of tribal leaders. In the early twentieth century, the founder of the modern Saudi state, Ibn Saud, cobbled together parts of the Arabian Peninsula, piecemeal, starting from his family's ancestral home of Riyadh and expanding outward to reclaim the two holiest cities of Islam, Mecca and Medina, until he finally consolidated the kingdom in 1932.

Ibn Saud's people included nomadic Bedouins, traders, pearl divers, farmers. For many of them, life had not changed for centuries. In his unprecedented conquest, he was both supported by and saddled with a group of ultraconservative clerics who had legitimized his royal family, the House of Saud, almost two centuries ago. These Wahhabi clerics were provincial and almost anti-modern: when the wireless telegraph was introduced in

24 Riyadh in the 1920s for instance, they inspected it for demons. The country developed a modern nation-state apparatus from scratch. Its first-ever national budget was issued in 1934 and most of its revenues came from *hajj* pilgrimage taxes.

But in 1938, American prospectors found oil in the kingdom's Eastern Province and everything changed. The kingdom began a sprint toward modernity that would see it develop a government, national idea, foreign policy, and international religious mission by the end of the century. Once a sort of backwater—in a Muslim world that was home to such dazzling capitals as Damascus and Cairo—Saudi Arabia saw the windfall beneath its sands as a divine gift, a chance for the birthplace of Islam to become the leader of the Muslim world. Today, many people recognize some of the attributes of Saudi-style religion without knowing its exact contours, such as intolerance of religious minorities or restrictive attitudes toward women's behavior. Or they might know vaguely that Saudi religion has been linked to Al Qaeda, 9/11, or ISIS. But that we know it at all is remarkable. No one would have expected it just a century ago.

A Desert Preacher

Like *neoliberal* and *hipster*, *Wahhabi* is a descriptor used almost exclusively by people who do not belong to the group. Wahhabism is a movement within Sunni Islam named after Muhammad ibn Abd al-Wahhab, an eighteenth-century preacher from central Arabia who sought to purify his faith of the idolatrous and blasphemous practices that he thought corrupted the austere monotheism at the heart of Islam. Wahhabism is the reason why the House of Saud can justify ruling the Arabian Peninsula.

Ibn Abd al-Wahhab's starting point was a concept called *tawhid,* the oneness of God. It is basically the Islamic notion of monotheism and affirming tawhid is the first part of the profession of Muslim faith: "There is no God but Allah." Simple enough, and all Muslims affirm this. But Wahhab conceptualized tawhid in a unique way that entailed rejecting all manner of shrines, saints, and rituals, and declaring every Muslim who felt differently to be an idolator or unbeliever. From the start, Wahhabism was tied to persecution, expansion, and conquest, particularly into the holy lands of Mecca and Medina, which are in a region called the Hejaz. Abd al-Wahhab and his troops waged dozens of battles in and around the region and, in the process, destroyed the shrine on the Prophet Muhammad's birthplace and the tomb of his wife Khadijah, burned Sufi books, looted the Prophet's tomb, and plundered the Shia holy site of Karbala in Iraq.

In 1744, Abd al-Wahhab vowed his loyalty to the tribal leader Muhammad bin Saud in a power-sharing agreement: Abd al-Wahhab would be in charge of religious matters and Muhammad bin Saud in charge of political ones. Wahhab would be free to preach across Arabia, and his mission of purifying Arabian Islam would be adopted by the House of Saud. Their agreement led to the formation of the first Saudi state that same year. Wahhabism continued to be the spiritual backbone of two more Saudi states, the last of which was consolidated in 1932 and remains in place today.

Wahhabis are intimately concerned with small things: the roles and dress of women, the way to hold your hands in prayer, the avoidance of music. Discouraged practices are called *shirk,* polytheism, or *bidah,* harmful innovations to the true religion.

26   The kingdom's clerics often issue *fatawa*, or legal opinions, forbidding such behaviors as celebrating the new millennium (1999) and taking photos with cats (2016). Other Wahhabi clerics active online maintain that crucifixion is "at some level eternally" valid as a punishment. These people have been dragged kicking and screaming into the twenty-first century, which has forced them to accept innovations like the internet and television inside the kingdom. Despite their idiosyncratic local context, Saudi scholars' fatwas are still actively sought by Salafis in places like Indonesia, so they have a global reach as well.

But the Wahhabi clerics, called *ulama*, are not all-powerful. Their influence has waxed and waned and was likely at its peak in the 1980s. Ultimately, "it's not a power-sharing agreement today," said Dr. Saad al-Faqih, a Saudi intellectual who lives in exile in London. "The king and the royal family hold the reins. They can arrest or push out ulama whenever they want. It's an extremely powerful and unaccountable state." He should know— he was relentlessly pursued by the kingdom for his reform activism in the 1990s and at one point even forcibly anesthetized before he managed to flee and seek asylum, like many Saudis, in London. "Do you know how long it took the ulama to approve American forces during the Gulf War [of 1990–91]?" he asked me. "A development that directly contradicts every Wahhabi doctrine about the sacredness of the Arabian Peninsula? Twelve hours."

Today, Wahhabi ulama have a less sympathetic leader in the hot-headed young Crown Prince Muhammad bin Salman, who has jailed or dismissed any clerics who fail to show total obedience to him. (It's not the most conservative ideologues who have been dismissed, but those who haven't fallen into line with his bombastic national agenda.)

Wahhabism is often referred to interchangeably with Salafism, but they are distinct movements. Salafism arose in the late nineteenth and early twentieth centuries in Egypt, where revivalist thinkers led by Mohammad Abduh and Rashid Rida reacted to European colonialism in much of the Muslim world with a movement to return to the traditions of the *salaf,* the first three generations of Muslims. For them, the only way forward for Muslims was to look to the past. Salafis, especially Salafi men, are instantly recognizable, with untrimmed beards and a clean upper lip, short pants that end above their ankles, and modest sandals. They say that these are all *sunnah,* traditions endorsed by the Prophet.

The rhetoric of Salafism sent shock waves through the Muslim world and its texts were rapidly disseminated. While they are still distinct paths, Wahhabism and Salafism found some "elective affinities" in the twentieth century, allowing their communities to mix, and their practical expressions in much of the world today are similar. For instance, both groups value the puritanical medieval theologian Ibn Taymiyya (who, for instance, railed against the veneration of saints and visitation of tombs) and both criticize Sufi devotional practices.

The Call

When the House of Saud signed its pact with Muhammad ibn Abd al-Wahhab, it cosigned his Wahhabi dawa. *Dawa* literally means to call or invite, but in practice it refers to the wide range of proselytization activities available to any Muslim person or

28   institution. Since the modern Saudi state was formed long after
the pact, official Saudi foreign policy has always involved Wahhabi dawa. But the golden age of Saudi dawa was from 1973 to
1990, from the oil boom until the first Gulf War.

The reason for this spiritual efflorescence was mundane:
the price of oil exploded in 1973. During the Arab-Israeli War,
Arab oil-producing countries embargoed the nations supporting Israel and their revenues skyrocketed. This flush
period dovetailed with the global Cold War and Saudi religious investments often found common ground with American
anti-Communist exploits. So there was a perfect midcentury
storm when the Wahhabi clerics' goals to spread their version
of Islam, the kingdom's new oil wealth, its ambitious foreign
policy to create solidarity amongst Muslim peoples, and global
geopolitical alignments all came together.

Saudi Arabia's many agents of dawa include a state Dawa
Ministry; several huge charities headquartered in the kingdom
and headed by Saudi nationals; Saudi universities, especially
the Islamic University of Medina, which was purpose-built for
international students; and Saudi embassies abroad. Dawa is a
key priority of the Saudi Wahhabi clerical establishment, for
whom spreading *Wahhabiyya* is a raison d'etre. (This could likely
be said of any "clerical establishment," but no others have billions of dollars allocated to help them realize it, along with the
support of a governing class that would be illegitimate without
them.) Several Saudi monarchs have also made it a point to use
Islam in their foreign policy, starting with King Faisal in the
1960s. The golden age of Saudi dawa left legacy effects all over
the world. But this book isn't just a historical survey; Saudi
dawa is very much alive. Most of its key bodies, including the

dedicated national Dawa Ministry, the Muslim World League, the World Assembly of Muslim Youth, and the Islamic University of Medina, are still operating, and Saudi Arabia remains one of the richest countries in the Middle East. But it has had to adapt its messaging after 9/11 and the so-called War on Terror, which is why Saudi dawa now includes things like counterextremism centers and interfaith conferences too.

Saudi dawa typically produces Salafis and not Wahhabis, because Wahhabism is so site-specific to Saudi Arabia. But "Wahhabi" remains, across the world, a common insult lobbied by local Muslims against newly and/or visibly conservative Muslims. The presence of a Salafi community in the world does not necessarily imply Saudi dawa, because Salafism is now a truly global, transnational, and popular movement. Salafis are found in every sizable Muslim community from Pakistan to Cambodia to Kenya to the United States and there are many Salafisms adapted to their local contexts. For instance, doctrinaire Salafis are marked by an obsessive emphasis on the Quran and Hadith (the sayings attributed to the Prophet) and don't endorse any school of Islamic jurisprudence. But many Salafis today, especially those in or adjacent to political power, and certainly in all the countries visited in this book, tend to fuse Salafi precepts with their local legal traditions.

Why is Salafism so appealing? Acolytes cite its radical simplicity and democratic nature. It privileges direct access to texts, which at this point can easily be read online. Due to its transnational nature, Salafism offers a powerful sense of community all around the world. In countries where religious authority slowly became ritualized and siloed by elites, which is to say, nearly all of them, Salafism has a ready-made audience. And for Muslims

30 taking part in a religious revival after a prolonged period of religious suppression, like in Indonesia and Kosovo, Salafism tells you how to behave and what to do. As Drilon Gashi, an imam in Kosovo who studied in Medina, told me: "I had a lot of questions. And Salafis had a lot of answers."

An Islamic Foreign Policy

It's interesting to note that foreigners helped consolidate the Wahhabi mission in the Arabian Peninsula long before the kingdom started systematically exporting it. In the 1920s, hundreds of West Africans sought refuge from the "Antichrist," (i.e. their colonial rulers) in Mecca and Medina. Some of them became scholars and helped preach Wahhabism to unconverted Bedouin tribes in the desert. (It was no mean feat, as Bedouins were still known to terrorize pilgrims going from Mecca to Medina at the time.) So even the internal spread of Wahhabism, the backbone of the Saudi state, has long been an international project.

Given the difficulty of establishing his kingdom, Ibn Saud didn't seriously consider Islam as a part of his foreign policy. He did reopen the hajj to non-Wahhabis in 1925, but he was more interested in cementing the kingdom as a modern nation-state than in expanding the Wahhabi mission. His successor, King Saud bin Abdulaziz (who ruled from 1953 to 1964), was even less interested in proselytization; he almost bankrupted the kingdom, depleting the national treasury, at one point, to about $100.

It was only King Faisal, who ascended the throne in 1964, who saw the true potential of Saudi religion. And he had a fortuitous opportunity to stake his claim in geopolitics when Egypt's extremely popular leader Gamel Abdul Nasser, a proponent of socialism and pan-Arab unity, soundly lost the Arab-

Israeli War in 1967 and thus his bid for leadership of the Muslim world.

Under Faisal's watch, first as prince then as king of Saudi Arabia, the kingdom established most of its key international dawa bodies: the Muslim World League (MWL) in 1962, the Organization of Islamic Cooperation (OIC) in 1972, the World Assembly of Muslim Youth (WAMY) in 1972. They formed the backbone of a cosmopolitan postcolonial Muslim world, which had an international circuit somewhat like the Davos-to-Aspen thought leadership junket of today. Mohammad Siddik, an Indonesian Muslim scholar who got swept up in MWL and WAMY as an Indonesian delegate in the 1960s, remembers traveling from his small town in western Indonesia to Riyadh, Brussels, London, Jeddah, and New York. "We felt like we were building a new world for the *umma*," the global Islamic community, he recalled to me decades later.

The kingdom was building itself, too. Until 1951, there were only three ministries in its whole government: foreign affairs, finance, and defense. In 1954, there were ten, and by 1975, there were twenty-four. Wahhabi clerics were allowed to steer ministries like that of *waqf* (endowments), justice, and education. They also controlled the directorate of "religious research, Islamic legal rulings, Islamic propagation, and guidance," which supplied the content of weekly Friday sermons and distributed key Wahhabi texts; the directorate became a full-fledged Ministry of Islamic Affairs, Dawa, and Guidance in 1993.

The Oil Boom

Despite Faisal's grand ambition, the Wahhabi message was not always well received. It was not even well formed at the time it

32   was exported. This is important because there is a tendency to assign a coherent global goal to Saudi dawa, but in reality it was half-baked at nearly every juncture. Were it not for the belated boost of oil wealth in the 1970s, it likely never would have resonated abroad. Even though Saudi Arabia is the birthplace of Islam, there were hardly any scholars of note from there in the early twentieth century, when most of the famous authors and imams came from countries like Egypt and Syria.

The kingdom overcame this handicap with reams of cash. The year 1973 was its turning point; after that year's oil embargo, its revenues curved exponentially. They went from about $10 million a year in 1946 to about $2 billion in 1971 to $22.6 billion in 1974, peaking at $113.3 billion a year in 1981. As oil wealth flooded the conservative kingdom, it inhabited its own identity more confidently. During this period, domestic religious police doubled down on internal laws against mixed-gender socializing, singing the Quran melodically, and depicting women on TV.

In 1979, two key events consolidated Saudi Arabia's international ambitions. First, the Iranian Revolution broke out in February and immediately became the most successful expression of political Islam of all time. The Shia regime and Iran's superstar status in the Islamic world deeply threatened Saudi Arabia, which worried about a sort of domino effect of revolution-fever and Shia conversions. (Both were troublesome: a popular revolution would topple the Saudi monarchy, and Shiism would challenge its Sunni clerical establishment.) A few months later, armed civilians from Saudi Arabia itself tried to occupy the Great Mosque in Mecca and accused the clergy of not being pious enough. Juhayman's revolt, as it came to be

called, deeply rattled the monarchy. So it was no coincidence
that Saudi dawa skyrocketed in the 1980s.

At the same time, the kingdom started to heavily fund the
insurgent Afghan guerrillas in the Soviet-Afghan War of 1979
to 1989. They recast it as a holy war, or *jihad*, capturing the Saudi
imagination. Many young Saudis joined the guerrillas as foreign
fighters, while some went as "jihad tourists" on short excur-
sions that included photo ops holding a gun. Meanwhile, the
Wahhabi clerics were given even more rope at home and steered
the education and dawa ministries to further their agenda.

In 1982, King Fahd succeeded King Khalid. Despite a hedo-
nistic reputation earned in his youth, he, too, came to recognize
the power of piety. He tripled the budget of the Committee to
Prevent Vice and Promote Virtue and "Islamized" the curricula
of all the Saudi universities. Even within the kingdom, preachers
seemed to have more money and the religious police in particular were buttressed with cash. Under Fahd, wrote the historian
Robert Lacey, "the petrodollar went pious." It's no coincidence
that Faisal's and Fahd's names are still all over the Muslim world
today, fingerprints of the dawa of their age.

The Saudi Octopus

In 1982, David Ottaway, an American correspondent for the
Washington Post, was smuggled via private plane and car by the
Lebanese businessman Rafiq Hariri into the holy city of Medina.
Lying flat in Hariri's back seat, he became the first foreigner to
see the new King Fahd Complex for Printing the Holy Quran.
Estimated to cost $130 million, the plant was a royal pet project
in service of Fahd's global vision for Saudi Islamic diplomacy.
His complex sponsored the first major new edition of the Quran

34 since 1926. It would soon print millions of them to distribute both to hajj pilgrims and all around the world.

"I was stunned by the facility," Ottaway told me. "At the time, Fahd was in search of religious rehabilitation from his playboy image. He was probably the most tarnished of the kings." Ottaway himself, despite his transgression as a non-Muslim into Medina, was gifted an English-language Quran, which was edited by the General Presidency of Islamic Researchers, based on a translation by the British-Indian scholar Abdullah Yusuf Ali and revised through four committees to include page-by-page commentary and new "best expressions and fresh expressions" to spruce up the text. Some versions proposed, for instance, that non-Salafis are "hated by Allah" and that "Judgment Day will not come until Muslims will fight the Jews, and Muslims will kill all the Jews."

These days, the King Fahd Complex prints over 3.5 million Arabic-language Qurans and 387,000 translated Qurans in 16 different languages each year. They are sent off to six continents. Inside the kingdom, the center also runs workshops for prisoners to memorize the Quran. The Quran complex is run by the Saudi Ministry of Islamic Affairs, Dawa, and Guidance, which is one of the major arms of the state dawa apparatus. It works in concert with its local outposts and parallel to multinational charities and independent businessmen to transmit Saudi religious influence from the Gulf to Muslims around the world. Together these interlocking bodies form a sort of octopus reaching out from Arabia, with similar basic goals but freedom of movement at each end.

It was also King Fahd who created the influential institution of the "religious attaché" at Saudi embassies, which is a

diplomatic office responsible for in-country Wahhabi dawa and
building new mosques in host countries. One of the most influential today is found in Indonesia. They were funded to the tune of $27 billion, with a royal directive from King Fahd that said, "No limit should be put on expenditures for the propagation of Islam."

Keep in mind that Saudi revenues flow directly to the royal family and are not reported to anyone, and that most of their subsidiary organs' budgets are self-reported, so all figures related to their work must be taken with a grain of salt. The Ministry of Islamic Affairs, Dawa, and Guidance maintains its undisclosed budget today through the kingdom's *waqf,* or charitable endowment. Beyond this, the big three charities are the Muslim World League (MWL), the World Association of Muslim Youth (WAMY), and the International Islamic Relief Organization (IIRO). Their budgets have been estimated to be in the tens of millions per year, but no exact figures have ever been released.

The Dawa Ministry has a staff of over 9,500 people in the kingdom and oversees religious diplomacy in about two dozen countries in Europe, Asia, Africa, the Middle East, Australia, and the US. It is also responsible for dawa and the maintenance of mosques inside the kingdom. It had an operating budget of over $1.86 billion, as of 2017. It keeps scrupulous yet inscrutable tabs on its foreign activities, which seem to be self-reported by its constituent overseas offices. These activities include TV, radio, newspaper, and magazine content; as well as courses, lectures, missionary and conversion activities, preaching, prison visits, seminars, camps, preaching tours (all counted in absolute units instead of, say, money expended); and distributing Qurans, Quran commentaries, pamphlets, and cassettes in both Arabic

36 and in translations. For the Islamic year* 2016–17, its activities included sponsoring 22,146 conversions to Islam, 16,644 seminars, 43,303 preaching tours, and 374,454 classes or lectures around the world.

The ministry has been led by Sheikh Abdullatif bin Abdulaziz Al-Sheikh since 2018. He has distinguished himself as an opponent of political Islam à la the Arab Spring. The activities of Saudi religious attachés abroad also fall within its mandate. Beyond the ministry are the flagship Saudi charities, which are typically endowed by Saudi royals at their discretion and are often staffed by Saudis who have held prominent political posts. For instance, the current Secretary-General of the Muslim World League used to have a cabinet appointment as the Minister of Justice. Saudi charity budgets also typically have leeway for private donors, so they are even more opaque than the Dawa Ministry. As an example, the official Saudi Red Crescent budget for 2002 was about $10 million, but its revenues that year were actually about $66 million, due in part to obscure private donors.

The big Saudi charities are headquartered inside the kingdom and work through hundreds of local affiliates. For instance, if you want Saudi funding for a mosque, you could create a small association or institute on the spot, seek a letter of recommendation from the local office of the Muslim World League, and wait for them to disburse funds from their national

---

* Islamic lunar years, slightly shorter than Gregorian calendar years, are calculated in time elapsed since the Hijra, when the Prophet Muhammad and his followers migrated from Mecca to Medina and established the first Muslim community in AD 622.

budget or from Gulf donors. In Indonesia today, MWL is headquartered in Jakarta but has over thirty local outposts.

The most important international Saudi charity, the Muslim
World League, was created in Mecca in 1962 and authorized
by the grand mufti of Saudi Arabia to proselytize Wahhabi
Islam around the world, help oppressed Muslim minorities, and
"combat Sufism and religious innovations." In 1974, its stated
annual budget was $50 million. After the Iranian Revolution in
1979, the MWL was a key proponent of Saudi-style Sunni Islam
in direct opposition to Shia Islam, under the leadership of the
stringent Wahhabi ideologue Abd al-Aziz ibn-Baz, commonly
shortened to "Bin Baz." Bin Baz was the preeminent Wahhabi scholar of the twentieth century and generated the now-
infamous fatwas prohibting women from driving cars and autho-
rizing jihad in Afghanistan. By 1987, MWL had thirty offices
worldwide and a dedicated body called the Supreme World
Council of Mosques. It also dispatched nearly a thousand missionaries and paid for the hajj of a thousand pilgrims per year.

Its budget mainly draws from the Saudi royal family's endowment; small portions are also contributed by businessmen and ordinary people's donations. In March 1997,
the Secretary-General of MWL said the Saudi government
had given it over $1.33 billion since its founding. MWL can be
described as state-adjacent and its staffers sometimes get diplomatic passports.

MWL immediately became a player on the international
stage. Within the ideological currents of the postwar twentieth
century, it most directly opposed the emergent Third World
nationalism, promoting pan-Islamic solidarity in place of

38   secular nation-building. Soon after it was founded, then-Prince
      Faisal traveled to Washington, D.C., to explain the League's
      goals and its potential as a "bulwark against Communism." Its
      greatest impacts in this respect were in Afghanistan and Paki-
      stan, where it was heavily involved in anti-Soviet activity. At
      the same time, the discourse inside MWL circles was fairly eru-
      dite; one volume of essays published from its 1987 annual con-
      ference calls for an intellectual renaissance in the Islamic world,
      and another from the same year includes an essay by a British
      Muslim convert named Aisha Lemu calling for women to be
      actively included in proselytization.

          The World Assembly of Muslim Youth (WAMY) is another
      important semi-governmental charity. It is regulated by the
      Dawa Ministry and is considered somewhat more hardline than
      the MWL. The International Islamic Relief Organization (IIRO)
      was established in 1978 and focused on refugees and relief
      operations after wars and natural disasters. In 1997, its fund-
      raising target, under Prince Salman's oversight, was $266.6 mil-
      lion. Nearly half its funds went to terrorist training camps in
      Afghanistan and Kashmir in the 1980s. It also pledged support
      to Osama bin Laden when he started Al Qaeda and its offices
      abroad overlapped with the terrorist organization. Its Albania
      office, for instance, was staffed by regional Al Qaeda affili-
      ates and its branch in the Philippines funded the militant Abu
      Sayyaf group.

          The Saudi Red Crescent, an Islamic variant of the Red
      Cross charity, was founded in 1933 and has fourteen branches
      in the kingdom and more than 3,000 paid staff. It has been
      active in many of the high-profile conflicts involving Muslim

communities of the last three decades, including Afghanistan, Chechnya, Kosovo, and Palestine.

According to King Fahd's legacy website, in the three decades of his reign from 1982–2005, the kingdom spent four billion Saudi riyal, or over $1 billion, on mosques, schools, preachers and teachers' salaries, scholarships, and textbooks, which went toward at least 1,500 mosques, 200 Islamic centers, 200 colleges, and 2,000 schools or madrasas. This included at least $10 million to build mosques in the US.

Thanks in part to this massive effort, Muslims around the world could consume the same Wahhabi and Salafi books and tapes and Saudi-explicated Qurans, often in their own language, en masse. Saudi Arabia's proselytizing energies coincided with the rise of cheap mass media, and cassette tapes, in particular, became an important conduit for Wahhabi sermons. Today, the same small corpus of authors is still found in Salafi bookshops around the world: the medieval theologian Ibn Taymiyya; the movement's founder, Muhammad ibn Abd al-Wahhab; the Albanian scholar Muhammad Nasiruddin al-Albani. A book typical of this effort is a collected volume of Islamic rulings of Bin Baz, in which you may find his motley opinions like that the translation of Greek philosophy is evil, that one must not drink from containers made of gold or silver, that it is impossible to atone for engaging in anal sex, that women should not leave the house wearing perfume, and so on. Ironically, photocopying is theoretically forbidden by Salafi doctrine (as a form of theft), but it's nonetheless ubiquitous in Salafi communities and helped these texts spread even faster. In the 1980s, after the Iranian Revolution, anti-Shiism became a mainstay of Saudi dawa materials.

40   Beyond the big four charities are hundreds more small ones; in 2002 there were 264, by one count, with combined assets of $550 million, from both private donors and state subsidies. Dr. Ali bin Ibrahim al-Namlah, the former Minister of Labour and Social Affairs, said the Saudi government subsidized about 80 percent of these charities' expenditures and the cost of building their headquarters.

One of the most notorious minor charities is the Al-Haramain Islamic Foundation (AHIF). It was founded later than the big four charities, in 1988. As of 2003, it had printed 15 million copies of Islamic books, established more than 1,100 mosques and schools, and dispatched more than 3,000 missionaries abroad. It spent about $50 million a year on the tail end of the Afghan jihad in the 1980s. In 2000, AHIF had forty branches in Saudi Arabia and more than a hundred offices abroad, mostly in Asia and Africa but also several in the Balkans, including in Bosnia, Kosovo, Albania, and Croatia. In the years leading up to 9/11, Al-Haramain used a centralized system by which no subsidiary could receive funds without the personal approval of the foundation's director, who was, at the time, a Saudi man named Shaykh Aqil Ibn Abdul-Aziz Al-Aqil. Through this central command, Al-Haramain has been linked to an all-star list of terrorist groups including Jemaah Islamiyah in Indonesia, Al-Ittihad Al-Islami in Somalia, Lashkar-e-Taiba in Pakistan, Chechen rebels, and, of course, Al Qaeda. From 2004 to 2010, the UN recommended its assets be blocked due to its Al Qaeda affiliations, but this proved incredibly difficult to enforce. Many of Al-Haramain's foreign offices opened and closed frequently in the 2000s, but it was impossible to eradicate completely. In Kosovo, I was told, it has operated under at least ten different names.

Other charities are pet projects of the kingdom's countless princes and princesses or were created ad hoc by its various
wealthy businessmen. The mysterious Islamic Benevolence
Committee was founded in 1987 by the Saudi businessman
Shaykh Adil Galil Abdul Batargee and kept an office in Planta-
tion, Florida, to solicit donations from American Muslims. It
was later linked to the militant Abu Sayyaf group in the Philippines and to terrorist plots in Bosnia. Many of the smaller charities utilize a paperless system of finance called *hawala* ("in trust")
to transfer money. Such transfers are one reason why Saudi
charities, even ones that were fairly official or state-endorsed,
so frequently became embroiled with terror finance.

Not every Saudi project succeeded. The Organization of
Islamic Cooperation, or OIC, was founded in 1969 to be like the
United Nations of the Islamic world. But because it's so big and
includes so many different kinds of states and so many specialized committees, it has been barely influential in any significant
historical development beyond eliciting solidarity for besieged
Muslim communities like those in the Bosnian and Kosovo Wars
and the Rohingya being subjected to genocide today in Myanmar.

The Most Special Relationship

Saudi ambitions for the Muslim world were vast, but not predes-
tined to succeed. At the Bandung conference of 1955, a remarkable assemblage of twenty-nine newly independent Asian and
African states, Crown Prince Faisal did not make much of a
splash. "An avuncular [Gamel Abdul] Nasser shepherded around
a cagey Faisal," in the words of the Marxist historian Vijay Prashad. The superstars of that assembly were the progressive, secular leaders of huge, new nations like Jawaharlal Nehru of India

42 and Sukarno of Indonesia. Even the leading Muslim clerics of the time were working to synthesize Islam and Communism. It seemed that the future would belong to these ambitious post-colonial dreamers, not a strange and closed Gulf monarchy. But over the course of the century, it was the Saudi vision that would triumph. One new nation after another abandoned its leftist and liberal dreams when faced down by political Islam and religious conservatism. It was not merely that Saudi Arabia's ideology was inherently more attractive, but that they picked the right partner to advance their ambitions for the century: the United States. When the new global hegemon and the oil-rich monarchy teamed up during the Cold War, their combined efforts were often unbeatable.

The US—Saudi relationship was forged between elites, as opposed to through organic, historic, or cultural ties. Its transactional nature was underscored by a mutual unintelligibility in the early years of their partnership. In the 1950s, American analysts for Aramco, the Saudi oil company, described Wahhabis as "Muslim Unitarians" to help American WASPs understand their worldview. (This seized on a real parallel between the Wahhabi concept of tawhid and the Unitarian belief that the Christian God is one person and not a Trinity, but elides much of the intolerant practical applications of the former.) Despite the current received wisdom that Saudi fundamentalism has been deleterious for the Muslim world, the intellectual consensus of the 1960s was exactly the opposite. President Eisenhower, for instance, exactly echoed the Saudi line that the West and Western ideas had in fact corrupted Islam—which explained the socialist agitation in places like Egypt—and Saudi influence could steer it back on course.

In the 1970s, Saudi Arabia became newly flush with oil
revenues to invest in foreign causes of its choice. Many of its
investments focused on anti-Soviet and anti-Communist
operations. By one 1977 estimate, the kingdom spent over $6
billion in foreign aid to countries involved in the tug of the Cold
War like Egypt, Pakistan, Syria, and Somalia. The proselytization
component of Saudi aid in these theaters did not concern the US.
If anything, conservative Islam was considered a useful counter-
weight to Communism. It was a time of which Henry Kissinger
wrote in his memoirs: "Often I found through other channels a
helpful Saudi footprint placed so unobtrusively that one gust of
wind could erase its traces."

Saudi Arabia, of course, opposed Communism and leftism
on its own terms and was not merely a pawn of the US. Those
popular ideologies would deeply threaten the power of the monarchy if they even caught on with the Saudi public. Saudi Arabia
became a key member of the whimsical-sounding Safari Club in
1976, an alliance founded by a French count between Iran, Egypt,
Saudi Arabia, Morocco, and France to counter Communism
in Africa. It was named after the group's first meeting place, a
Kenyan ranch owned by the Saudi arms dealer Adnan Khashoggi.
The group went on to execute a military intervention in Zaire
and provide arms to Somalia against Ethiopia before disbanding
in 1979, when the Iranian Revolution happened.

The US actively encouraged the Saudis to fund Islamist
militants against their shared enemies of the Islamic Republic
of Iran and the USSR. Washington saw the kingdom's lack of
financial transparency as an advantage. The US also played a
useful role in developing the kingdom's Islamic banking system,
which would become another instrument of international

44   influence. Banks including Citigroup, Price Waterhouse, and
      Chase Manhattan, as well as Chicago School economists like
      Milton Friedman, all provided training and technology to the
      kingdom in the 1970s.

      The peak phase of US–Saudi harmony in the global the-
      ater was during the Soviet-Afghan war, when Saudi Arabia's
      government spent an estimated $3 billion, not including con-
      siderable additional activity by the big Saudi charities, to sup-
      port the Afghan mujahideen. Saudi Arabia and President Jimmy
      Carter's administration agreed in 1980 to match each other's
      contributions to the Afghan cause roughly dollar-for-dollar.
      Saudi charities including MWL and the Red Crescent energet-
      ically supported the Palestinian jihadist Dr. Abdullah Azzam,
      the spiritual leader of the Afghan jihad, whose motto was, "Jihad
      and the rifle alone: no negotiations, no conferences, and no dia-
      logues." At the war's end in 1989, Azzam noted that "his organi-
      zation never lacked for funds because [the Saudi Red Crescent
      Society] headed by Prince Salman Abdel Aziz had a budget of
      $27 million per year."

      What did Saudi Arabia displace when it became a leader
      of the Muslim world, with Western support, in the 1980s?
      Arab nationalism, socialism, secularism, progressivism. Saudi
      Arabia bet on religion and political quietism instead of pro-
      gressive Muslim organizing and thus reshuffled the religious
      landscape of the Muslim world. Saudi foreign policy helped
      sublimate the revolutionary anti-imperialist energies of the
      postcolonial world into religion. Despite rumblings of discon-
      tent at home and a chaotic monarchy, it eventually managed to
      project a pious empire all around the world.

"Iran is a useful cover," said Bruce Riedel, a former CIA station chief and National Security Advisor to four US presidents.
"Saudis don't like to be called leader of the counterrevolution in
the Arab world, but that's what they are."

A Missionary University

In 1961, King Faisal fulfilled an Ottoman-era dream to build
a university in Medina, the second holiest city of Islam, from
where the message of Islam spread throughout the world. The
Islamic University of Medina, or IUM, is one of the most unique
instruments of Saudi dawa, and its graduates have shaped all
three of the countries covered in this book. Graduates of IUM
in the Muslim world are almost as ubiquitous as Stanford graduates in Silicon Valley. The university's letter to outgoing graduates in 1976 called on them to ascend "the stage of jihad in the
battalions of the dawa to your Lord."

The university opened its doors to the Muslim world well
before the Saudi oil boom, and it had an international orienta-
tion from the start. By 1967, just five years into operation, it had
scholarship students from Nigeria, Indonesia, Yugoslavia, Palestine, Jordan, and South Vietnam. By the 1980s, over two thousand Muslims from ninety different countries were studying
there, and in many developing countries, it was common to see
young Muslim men flocking to Saudi embassies in hopes of getting an IUM scholarship. IUM helped address the inconvenient
fact that Saudi scholars were never prominent internationally,
which seriously hampered their bid to define orthodoxy in the
Muslim world. The kingdom solved this problem, as does any
group with a talent deficit, with immigrants.

46   Over 60 percent of the university's inaugural staff was for-eign. It was a refuge for members of the Muslim Brotherhood Islamist movement who were driven out from Egypt in the 1960s and its secretary-general from 1978 to 1983 was Nigerian. One of the main Saudi citizens there was the Wahhabi cleric Bin Baz, who served as its second president. IUM started out with just 3,500 students in the 1990s and today it has about 16,000, which is mid-sized, but there are universities three or four times its size in Saudi Arabia. But its international influ-ence is matchless. In all the countries studied in this book, IUM alumni have become leading Salafi voices, Islamist politicians, influential preachers, and scholars. In Nigeria, IUM directly recruited promising students on annual tours throughout the 1970s and 1980s. In Indonesia, promising students at LIPIA, a Saudi university in Jakarta, were often offered scholarships to continue postgraduate study at IUM. Even before Kosovo became a country, Yugoslav students were studying in Medina on scholarships.

IUM's curriculum focused on religion to the exclusion of worldly sciences and expressed frequent concerns with reli-gious innovations and deviance. The founding vice president of IUM asserted that the earth, and not the sun, was at the center of the universe, which was a popular Wahhabi belief.

Later, Umm Al-Qura University in Mecca and Imam Muhammad ibn Saud University in Riyadh joined IUM's ranks as Islamic universities offering places to foreign stu-dents. And in just a few decades, Saudi Arabia's Islamic uni-versities competed with the likes of Al-Azhar, the illustrious thousand-year-old university in Cairo. Since only so many stu-dents could or would study abroad, Saudi Arabia funded several

other like-minded institutions abroad including the International University of Africa in Sudan (which opened its doors
in 1977), LIPIA in Jakarta (1980), and the Islamic University of
Niger (1986).

Under the Microscope

If you recognize the term "Wahhabi" or "Wahhabism," it's probably because of 9/11. In the wake of that attack, institutions like
Freedom House began to publish reports about "Wahhabi ideology" that seemed to provide some intellectual backing for a
senseless event. The same goes for Salafism, for which there
wasn't even a standard spelling in 2001: *The Guardian* went with
"Salafee" in one post-9/11 article.

The Saudi brand started to deteriorate a decade earlier,
during the Gulf War of 1990–1991, which ended the golden
age of its dawa. That was when Saddam Hussein attacked the
kingdom as an "American protectorate" for allowing US troops
on its holy land. The first World Trade Center attack in 1993
also drew scrutiny to Saudi charities, and that same year, the
Saudi government passed a law requiring all donations collected
by charities to be deposited in a fund administered by a Saudi
prince (though it was basically unenforceable). But 9/11 was
something else. Fifteen out of the nineteen hijackers were Saudi
nationals and popular opinion of the kingdom quickly soured.
Just six months after the attack, 54 percent of Americans agreed
that "the Kingdom of Saudi Arabia is a state that supports terrorism." The Gulf War was a blow to Saudi Arabia's bid for leadership of the Muslim world, but 9/11 brought it to its knees.

In 2002, the Council on Foreign Relations released a
strongly worded report condemning Saudi "terror financing,"

48   and the 9/11 Commission's much-awaited 2004 report called
out several Saudi charities like Al-Haramain in connection with
Al Qaeda. (The same report concluded, in a somewhat defeated
tone, that freezing terror financiers "appeared to have little
effect and, when confronted by legal challenges, the United
States and the United Nations were often forced to unfreeze
assets.") The idea of a dangerous, mysterious "Wahhabi ideology" became part of popular discourse.

The 838-page-long Joint Inquiry into the 9/11 attacks published in 2002 contains a 28-page section on Saudi financing
that was never declassified. American politicians who were
allowed to read it have said it is damning. Former Senator Bob
Graham said, "They point a very strong finger at Saudi Arabia
being the principal financier." Laurent Murawiec, a RAND cor-
poration analyst, said in a statement typical of that era, that
Saudi Arabia is "the kernel of evil, the prime mover, the most
dangerous opponent" of the United States.

"In the past we may have been naive in our giving," admitted
the Saudi government, in 2002, "and [we] did not have adequate
controls over all of our donations." Prince Bandar, then the
Saudi ambassador to the US, admitted, in a PBS *Frontline* interview in 2001: "You go to Friday prayers. You could stand there
and say, 'Please help.' And people will give you checks, money,
et cetera."

Something else happened while Saudi Arabia was in the
spotlight: it experienced a 9/11 of its own. Al Qaeda, led by the
Saudi national Osama bin Laden, attacked major targets in the
kingdom, destroying a housing compound in Riyadh in 2003
and then Saudi oil fields in 2004. Bin Laden, who was once a

valued partner of the Saudi government in Afghanistan, also turned against the kingdom during the 1991 Gulf War. After these attacks transpired on its own soil, Saudi Arabia could no longer really afford to ignore its links to terror financing and it launched an intense counterextremism initiative in earnest. The US and Saudi Arabia once again became reluctant partners in this so-called War on Terror. Their partnership no longer had the ideological zeal of the Cold War and much bad blood had been shed. But they needed each other.

The Saudi government set up a joint task force with the US to investigate terrorist financing, and in May 2003, introduced banking regulations that temporarily stopped all private charities from sending funds abroad. These shock waves would be felt around the Muslim world, where Saudi charity had become an integral part of the educational and development layers of society. In 2003, the kingdom briefly considered recalling its religious attachés. In 2004, a royal decree was issued to centralize charities.

Thus, 9/11 briefly imploded the transnational Saudi dawa apparatus. Restrictions on foreign transfers led to a 40 percent drop in donations to the World Assembly of Muslim Youth, said its leader, Saleh S. Al Wohaibi, in 2010. Saudis who wanted to donate to WAMY could not merely transfer money to well-publicized bank accounts but had to do it in person and get a receipt. It was during this freeze that Salafis in countries like Indonesia and Nigeria started to find their own footing and develop their own regional vernaculars.

One weak link revealed after 9/11 was the phenomenon of independent Saudi businessmen who funded Al Qaeda. In a

50   report prepared for the UN in December 2002, the independent
      security analyst Jean-Charles Brisard listed nine Saudi bankers
      and businessmen by name as financial sponsors of Al Qaeda.

      It was also in the post-9/11 era that the American fixation
      with Saudi textbooks began. After dialogues in 2003 and 2006,
      Saudi Arabia revised about 5 to 10 percent of curricula and
      textbooks that were flagged for intolerance, including passages
      about denouncing unbelievers and idolators. Saudi textbooks
      were once again subject to a highly publicized congressional
      review in 2015 when the specter of the Islamic State emerged.
      Problematic passages included those addressing Jews, Chris-
      tians, "infidels," minority Muslim sects, the status of women,
      homosexuals, and "apostasy or sorcery," according to a 2018
      review by the Anti-Defamation League. The ADL found that
      "stridently intolerant" material about Shia, Sufis, Jews, and
      Christians had decreased over the last decade in elementary-
      and middle-school textbooks. Such material is doubtless prob-
      lematic, but in the grander scheme of things, it does seem like
      a minor fixation.

The Paradox of Obedience

      Saudi Arabia's ambitions to define orthodoxy in the Muslim
      world, fight revolutionary ideologies coming from Iran and
      Egypt, and support besieged Muslim minorities stretched it into
      a global campaign by the 1990s that frankly outpaced its capac-
      ities. That's why the quality and impact of Saudi organs today
      varies so wildly, from a muscular religious attaché's office in
      Jakarta to a one-person Muslim World League outpost in Nigeria.

      It's not a straightforward cause-and-effect. Nothing shows
      this better than the trajectory of Osama bin Laden himself. Born

into a Saudi family of construction millionaires, he was the face of the lavishly Saudi-funded Afghanistan jihad in the 1980s, but within a decade, he became so disillusioned with the House of Saud as to bomb the kingdom. Bin Laden is among hundreds of Saudi youth who tried to fight their jihads all around the world, in places like Afghanistan, Chechnya, Kashmir, Bosnia, Somalia, and eventually the US. For the eminent Saudi scholar Madawi al-Rasheed, who lives in self-imposed exile in London, the phenomenon of Saudi jihadis perfectly encapsulates the tension between the kingdom's rhetoric to "obey their current rulers at home while at the same time fostering the spirit of jihad abroad."

That gets to the heart of why Saudi dawa has such chaotic effects outside the kingdom's borders, where Saudi royals have no authority, and Wahhabism is stripped of its tentpole. Overseas, Saudi dawa typically manifests as transnational Salafism, not Wahhabism per se. Saudi charity has ended up supporting seemingly opposed causes abroad: political Islamists as well as jihadists, self-contained Salafi enclaves as well as vigorous missionaries, humble village mosques as well as ones that become hotbeds of extremism.

Does Saudi dawa actively create terrorists? Sometimes, but in very specific conditions, like the Afghan jihad, when it sponsored Abdullah Azzam and Osama bin Laden. Has Saudi dawa inspired terrorists, jihadists, and extremists? Much more broadly, yes. But they are one of many beneficiaries.

"Salafi-jihadism," the strain of violent Salafism that includes Al Qaeda, Boko Haram, ISIS, and more, has been resilient over the past three decades, as the scholar Shiraz Maher writes in *Salafi-Jihadism*. Salafi-jihadism typically draws from a larger pool of nonviolent Salafis, and those are often a direct

52   result of Saudi dawa. In Indonesia, Nigeria, and Kosovo, regional Salafi movements have been directly and definitively supported by Saudi dawa.

Today, the most prominent Salafi-jihadist group, ISIS, claims to be the world's true Wahhabi state, and it set up its own printing press in Mosul in 2014 to publish Ibn Abd al-Wahhab's texts. The surprisingly widespread phenomenon of destroying ancient holy sites from Palmyra to Timbuktu follows a distinctly Wahhabi logic. ISIS is the worst offender, but non-jihadists do this, too: in Bale, Ethiopia, Saudi-affiliated fundamentalists destroyed more than thirty Sufi shrines in the early 2000s. The world's growing anti-Shia rhetoric, too, speaks in the distinctly Wahhabi language of "deviance" and "polytheism." And blasphemy convictions often echo the logic of *takfir,* "excommunicating" improper Muslims. Thus, circulation of Wahhabi ideas and texts has had far-reaching effects. It is remarkable that the ideas of one eighteenth-century Arabian preacher have resonated so widely. Even if Saudi officials occasionally decry these violent effects, they are in a tight place given that these actions are completely in accordance with the ideas of the most famous Saudi preacher of all time.

So the central paradox of Saudi dawa is that many of the doctrines that long entailed stability within the kingdom have sowed discord outside it. As one Saudi intelligence official observed in 2005: "We encouraged our young men to fight for Islam in Afghanistan. We encouraged our young men to fight for Islam in Bosnia and Chechnya. We encouraged our young men to fight for Islam in Palestine. Now we are telling them you are forbidden to fight for Islam in Iraq, and they are confused."

Oil Money in the Archipelago

Indonesia's first Wahhabis came of their own accord in the early nineteenth century. They were called the Padris, and they were clerics who became enamored with the emerging Wahhabi movement when they went on hajj from their homes in South Sumatra to Mecca. When they came back home, they tried to impose sharia and correct the idolatrous excesses of their community, forcing women to wear veils and men to grow out their beards. Their conflict with traditional clerics and nobles escalated into a full-blown war that raged from 1803 to 1837, until the Padris were squashed with Dutch reinforcement. These Padri Wars prompted probably the first accounts of Westerners wringing hands over the "Arabization" of "innocent" and "peaceful" Indonesian Islam, which was a trope in the wartime dispatches of Dutch diplomats serving in the East Indies.

The Islam of Indonesia, a nation of over 15,000 islands that straddle the Equator, is often described as "tolerant" and syncretic. Islam came to the archipelago around the thirteenth century, likely through Arab traders, and the powerful rulers of

54   Java and Sumatra gradually converted from Hinduism or Buddhism to Islam. The islands of what is now Indonesia belonged to a larger archipelagic Muslim medieval world that included parts of modern-day Thailand, Malaysia, Singapore, the Philippines, and Cambodia. Indonesia is still home to the world's largest Buddhist temple—Borobudur, in Central Java—many Hindu temples, millions of Christians, and rich mystical and animist traditions. Many of these have colored *Islam Nusantara,* or Islam of the archipelago. For instance, there is a shrine atop Mount Kumukus in Central Java known for a ritual where Muslim pilgrims climb to the top every thirty-five days for seven months and have sex with other pilgrims, who are complete strangers, atop a graveyard, to precipitate a change in fortunes or good luck. The rite, which includes elements of Javanese myth and esoteric Hindu Tantra, is but one example of "only-in-Indonesia" Islam.

Indonesian Muslims' relationship to the Gulf, a far-off place toward which all of them prayed but which few of them got to see in person, has always been in flux. There were the Padris warriors in Sumatra at the turn of the nineteenth century. A little later, in the 1830s, one Javanese Muslim, Nawawi al-Bantani, fled Dutch colonization for Saudi Arabia and became the imam of the Grand Mosque of Mecca. In the 1910s, there were more hajj pilgrims than ever from Indonesia, but they were actually punished for showing an interest in Wahhabism, because Mecca had not yet been absorbed into Ibn Saud's reconquest and regional clerics forced Wahhabi-curious pilgrims to recant their beliefs at swordpoint. Today, Indonesia is allotted the world's largest hajj quota of 231,000 people per year.

In the decades leading up to independence from Dutch rule in 1945, Indonesians developed several conservative Muslim organizations, usually led by scholars who had gone on hajj, studied in Mecca, or both. They include Persatuan Islam (PERSIS), a Wahhabi-inspired conservative organization started in 1923 in West Java by several hajjis. Another was Muhammadiyah, an organization inspired by proto-Salafi Egyptians and established in Central Java, again by a hajji, in 1912. These early groups were not funded by Saudi Arabia, but their founders found Wahhabi ideas to be highly relevant to the "idolatrous" society they saw around them. Saudi charities would later find such groups to be natural partners in their dawa.

From the start, these groups spurred huge debates in Indonesia. The specter of Wahhabism in the 1920s prompted Indonesian Muslims to organize a "Committee on the Hejaz," that petitioned Ibn Saud not to destroy shrines in Mecca. They regrouped in 1926 as a domestic organization called Nahdlatul Ulama (NU), which is still a powerful civil society group in Indonesia today and claims, with a membership of over forty million people, to be the largest Muslim organization in the world. NU has served as the self-appointed face of "traditional" Indonesian Islam against the increasingly strong revivalist currents, many of them from Saudi Arabia, that would pulse through Indonesia over the course of the twentieth century.

Given the impact of Saudi investments in Indonesia, it is remarkable that Indonesia and Saudi Arabia didn't even have diplomatic relations for much of the 1960s. In 1963, Indonesian police raided the Saudi ambassador's residence in the hilly countryside south of Jakarta without an explanation, and the

56   ambassador left in a huff, leaving no formal relationship between the Suharto military dictatorship and the kingdom. Diplomatic ties were only repaired in 1967 thanks to a statesman manqué named Mohammad Natsir, the same man who would go on to almost single-handedly seed Saudi influence in the archipelago.

Natsir, an Islamic scholar from Sumatra, was the first prime minister of independent Indonesia. In 1958, Natsir joined a rebellion against the founding president, Sukarno, which failed, and he went into exile deep in the Sumatran jungle. He emerged in 1961 and was promptly jailed. His Islamist political party was also banned. When he was finally allowed to return to civil society in 1966, the former founding father was ignored and shunned by the new Suharto military dictatorship, which had come to power through a violent, CIA-backed coup in 1965. Every door slammed in his face. He would have no future in politics.

But he didn't retire from public life. The pious Natsir was distressed by how Muslim voices were being denied a political voice in a new nation whose citizenry was 90 percent Muslim. He resolved to target Indonesian hearts and minds, instead of their votes. "We are no longer preaching by means of politics, but engaging in politics through preaching," he said. "The result will be the same." What he meant was that he would cultivate grassroots Islamic activism instead of push for Islamic laws and political institutions. Saudi Arabia was delighted to help him do exactly that.

With his thick, square soda-bottle glasses and natty fusion outfits—a tailored suit with a black *peci* cap, or a crisp button-down shirt and tie with a sarong—Natsir became a Zelig of the midcentury Muslim world. He embarked on a personal,

nongovernmental campaign of *dakwah*, the Indonesianized   57
word for dawa, among his fellow Muslim citizens.

In 1967, he created Dewan Dakwah Islamiyah Indonesia
(DDII), the "Indonesian Islamic Dawa Council," which would
become the chief conduit for Saudi money into Indonesia. From
the start, DDII was closely affiliated with the Muslim World
League in Mecca. Natsir actually served as one of the League's
founding members and its global vice president. DDII was so
closely tied to MWL that the latter did not bother to open a separate office in Indonesia until after Natsir died in 1993.

Natsir visited Saudi Arabia in 1967 and met King Faisal, who
was just three years into his reign and was deeply impressed by
the pious emissary from the edge of the Muslim world. He kept
asking Natsir what he could do to help his dawa in Indonesia, and
Natsir replied: "Help my children." DDII was granted numerous
scholarships for Indonesian students to study in Medina. Until
his death in 1993, Natsir handpicked several students a year for
IUM. By the early 2000s, DDII still received twenty-five Saudi
scholarships per year to distribute among Muslim organizations in Indonesia.

Natsir's personal diplomacy won him an open-ended *tazkiya*, or recommendation letter, from Mecca to accept donations from any Saudi source. DDII became a vessel for other
Saudi dawa bodies like IIRO and WAMY. In the early 1980s, half
of the Supreme World Council of Mosques' $29 million budget
was designated for Southeast Asia. Due to Natsir's well-known
relationship with King Faisal, DDII became the bridge between
other conservative Islamic Indonesian organizations—like
Persis and Muhammadiyah—and Saudi Arabia.

58   He was most paranoid about Christian missionary activity in the new Indonesia and focused on preaching to existing Muslims. But with the influx of cash and exposure to the transnational aims of the MWL, DDII diversified its programming. It started to print a hugely popular monthly magazine called *Media Dakwah* and published translations of major Islamist authors like Egypt's Sayyid Qutb and Pakistan's Abu'l A'la Maududi, as well as the infamous anti-Semitic conspiracy theory *The Protocols of the Elders of Zion*. It also conducted intensive outreach on university campuses, sponsoring mosques and Islamic centers at twelve universities. These campus branches, in turn, introduced students to Islamist thought and became a feeder for future DDII members.

New paragraph: Natsir's work was happening at a true grassroots level. On the state level, Indonesia did not even seek membership in the Saudi-led Organization of Islamic States in 1972 and refused to sign its founding charter.

And all of this—Natsir's turn from politics to Islamic activism, his first meeting with King Faisal, the first Indonesian scholarship students in Medina, the beginnings of Saudi dawa in Indonesia—was taking place before the Iranian Revolution. That is, Indonesia was a ripe target, home to a huge and impressionable Muslim population in a new country, but it was not a battleground. It became one in 1979.

The Iranian Revolution hit Indonesia hard, recalls Nasir Tamara, an Indonesian who was on the plane with Ayatollah Khomeini from Paris to Tehran when he went to inaugurate the Islamic Republic of Iran on February 1, 1979. Tamara, who is originally from South Sumatra, was a graduate student in

philosophy at the Sorbonne in the 1970s when the Ayatollah
lived in the sleepy suburb of Neauphle-le-Château, giving
daily interviews to a horde of foreign journalists, presenting
himself as the mystical, populist leader of a country oppressed
by decadent, Western-backed royals. Tamara went to see the
Ayatollah in his exile, first out of curiosity, but soon as a correspondent for the *Sinar Harapan* newspaper in Jakarta. Indonesian readers were so crazy for updates on the percolating
revolution that every issue carrying one of Tamara's reports
had a double print run.

"At the time, the grip of Marxism was still very strong in
Europe and the idea of religion as a locomotive for a nation was
fascinating," reflected Tamara, now in his sixties, at his elegant bungalow in South Jakarta. "All eyes were on Iran." Iran was
the most important country in the Middle East then, he said,
not Saudi Arabia. Having built up a rapport, he was eventually
invited to join the Ayatollah on his return to Tehran, where he
and the other foreign journalists landed without any kind of
visa. (He claims he jumped over the airport walls to get to the
action.) Within a year, his reports had been collected and bound
into a bestselling book, *Revolusi Iran,* that's still in print today.

The revolution was not considered a Shia phenomenon at
the time, recalls Tamara, but a win for Muslims worldwide. Even
Mohammad Natsir was excited by the new regime, and the pro-
logue to Tamara's book was written by a DDII cadre. Many Indonesian Muslim intellectuals were invited to Tehran in the early
years of the revolutionary regime. Iranian books, like those by
the revolutionary ideologue Ali Shariati, were translated into
Indonesian and sold briskly, especially in university towns. "He

60   was like our Che Guevara," said Ulil Abshar-Abdalla, a Muslim intellectual who lives in Jakarta. "I read his book from cover to cover when I was in high school in Central Java."

College students across the country formed study circles to read Shia texts, and many young intellectuals converted to Shiism. The Iranian embassy in Jakarta published a magazine called *Yaum al-Quds*, distributed scholarships to study in the holy city of Qom, and held popular events celebrating Persian culture. Even Abdullah Sungkar, who would become one of Indonesia's most prominent jihadists, briefly tried to foment an Iran-inspired revolution in Central Java.

This all struck fear into the heart of Saudi Arabia. The very next year after the revolution, Saudi Arabia created a school by royal decree called Lembaga Pengajaran Bahasa Arab, the Arabic Language Teaching Institute, in Central Jakarta. Within five years, the language institute became a proper university and migrated to South Jakarta, where it remains today, and renamed itself as the Islamic and Arabic College of Indonesia, or LIPIA. LIPIA is a branch of Imam Muhammad bin Saud University in Riyadh; it was the first accredited foreign educational institution in Indonesia. Housed in a modern chrome-and-glass building, with signage all in Arabic and a rotating cast of foreign professors and Saudi directors in *thobes,* it made a big splash.

Around this time, DDII started to channel Saudi Arabia's anti-Shia agenda. There have never been many Shia in Indonesia, whose Muslims are about 99 percent Sunni, but nevertheless, DDII became a primary agent of the campaign against them. Its publications shifted from Muslim Brotherhood texts to anti-Shia screeds. It also published extensive, blow-by-blow coverage of the Soviet-Afghan war, where hundreds of Indonesians went to become foreign fighters in Saudi- and US-backed guerrilla units.

It's important to know the story of Mohammad Natsir and DDII because Saudi dawa isn't just about ideas or money, but about relationships. The success of Saudi proselytization in the twentieth century is due in large part to energetic royals like King Faisal and tireless partners like Mohammad Natsir in Indonesia. This is also why the Saudi project is much more dissolute and unfocused today: there is less concentrated will on both ends. In Indonesia, the legacy of the towering figure of Natsir remains important in the dawa infrastructure to this day.

Today, DDII is led by Mohammad Siddik, a scholar hand-picked as a cadre by Natsir in the 1990s. Siddik, now seventy-seven years old, grew up in Aceh, the ultraconservative, westernmost province of Indonesia. He is swarthy, with a clipped white beard, and speaks perfect, late-Raj-style English, a legacy of the cosmopolitan midcentury Muslim milieu through which he traveled, a world created in no small part by the transnational Saudi charity network.

Siddik graduated from college in Jakarta in 1967 and asked Natsir, whom he still considers to be "the father of our nation," for career advice. Natsir remembered that Siddik had visited him in jail and, as a reward for his loyalty, invited him to join the newly formed DDII. There was no typical day on the job. Once, in 1968, Siddik was sent as a delegate to a Muslim World League conference and ended up using his open-ended plane ticket to visit sundry capitals of the world: Prague, Kathmandu, London. He remembers walking down Pancasila Marg in Delhi, named after the political philosophy of Indonesia and inspired

62   by the friendship between the postcolonial leaders Sukarno and
      Nehru. He was impressed by the connection even though he
      thought then and now that secular-leaning Sukarno was "in the
      pocket of Communists." "We were all against the Communists
      then," he recalled. He also attended the inaugural conference of
      the World Assembly of Muslim Youth in 1972 in Riyadh.

      DDII is housed in an eight-story, star-shaped building,
      in Cikini, Central Jakarta. It has offices in thirty-two of the
      thirty-four provinces of Indonesia and forty people work in the
      Jakarta headquarters alone. (All are Indonesians.) Saudi funding
      has long since dried up, according to Siddik, and its revenues
      today come from the properties it owns through its charitable
      endowment.

      More than four decades after its founding, DDII has "both
      lost and won," said Ulil Abshar-Abdalla. The organization itself
      is less influential and well funded now than in the 1980s and
      1990s, when it raised the banner of opposition to Suharto's sec-
      ular authoritarian regime. But its ideas are now ensconced in
      the mainstream.

LIPIA

Abshar-Abdalla cuts an interesting figure through Indonesia's
religious landscape. Though now a prominent liberal intellectual, he actually studied at LIPIA from 1988 to 1993. As a teen-
ager in Pati, Central Java, Abshar-Abdalla placed first in an
Arabic class held at his local *madrasa*. The prize was six months
of tuition at LIPIA. At the end of those months, LIPIA offered
him another six. He stayed on. After that, it offered him four
more years of free tuition to obtain a bachelor's degree in sharia.
He accepted that too. He studied standard topics like theology,

jurisprudence, and the Quran; there were few electives. When
he went to collect his monthly cash allowances as an undergraduate, there was usually a donations box for the Afghan jihad. In
1993, when he was set to graduate, he was offered a scholarship
to continue his studies in Riyadh. And he finally said no.

"Once you accept that, you're on their payroll for life,"
Abshar-Abdalla told me, at his home in East Jakarta. "But they
made it awfully easy to stick around. I'm from a poor family, and
it was quite tempting. . . . I think they managed to pull a few good
minds from my generation that way."

What happened, instead, was that Abshar-Abdalla boomer-
anged in the other direction, recoiling at the Salafi and Wahhabi
theology that was mandatory for every year of his free university education. He went on to found the Liberal Islam Network
in 2001, a few years after democracy came to Indonesia in 1998.
It was in part a reaction to the hardline groups like the Islamic
Defenders Front. But his vocal criticism of Islamists elicited
vitriol, and in 2002, he was mailed a mysterious package filled
with wires at the office he rented in the Menara Ravindo tower.
He passed it off to security for inspection and the unwitting
policeman who opened it lost his arm. The bomb was meant for
Abshar-Abdalla.

"He was white as a ghost that day," recalls Andreas Harsono,
a human rights researcher in Indonesia, who worked in the
same building as Abshar-Abdalla at the time. He was assigned a
round-the-clock security detail, which followed him to Harvard,
where he had been admitted to do a PhD in theology. He never
finished the degree. "How could he?" said Harsono. "Imagine
writing a book when you can't even leave your apartment alone
to get coffee."

Abshar-Abdalla has a brusque manner that is unusual in Java. He has seen his Liberal Islam Network die a slow death, with nobody from the next generation interested in picking up the torch; many Indonesian youth are more religiously conservative than their parents. Embittered, at age fifty-two, he is now a sort of freelance public intellectual and made more enemies in 2016 when he came out as a supporter of the Islamist candidate for Jakarta governor, the one who defeated the Christian targeted by the Islamist protests. "What's the point?" became his governing ethos. He has since found some solace in working on topics in Sufi theology for a specialized audience, rather than lobbying a resistant general public.

But even he admits that Salafism was briefly seductive. "It was so straightforward," he said. "Much more clear-cut than the complex traditions I grew up with." Abshar-Abdalla has been a Cassandra figure, foreseeing a rise in Salafism and intolerance in Indonesia exactly like what he was taught at LIPIA. He has been proved right on many counts, but has almost paid with his life.

LIPIA is the most visible outpost of Saudi dawa in Indonesia. It is one of the biggest accomplishments of the peak dawa era worldwide, a brick-and-mortar university entirely administered by Saudis in the world's largest Muslim-majority country and, furthermore, one whose alumni have been disproportionately influential in Indonesian public life. LIPIA gives full scholarships to all its students today and its leadership is entirely Saudi and it is overseen by the embassy.

LIPIA's predecessor, the LPBA language institute, was set up by the Saudi ambassador at the time, Bakr Abbas Khamis. It taught Arabic in one- or two-year-long courses to promising

students—selected by DDII from prominent Islamic boarding
schools across Indonesia—who would be good candidates for
higher education in Saudi Arabia. In 1986, it became a full-
fledged university offering bachelor's degrees. Its first director,
the Saudi national Abd al-Aziz Abd Allah al-Amr, was a student
of the important Wahhabi cleric Bin Baz.

The classes are all still conducted in Arabic. There is barely
any Indonesian text even visible on campus. There are female
students, but they study in classrooms on a separate level
from the male students and watch video lectures that are
live-streamed from the male classrooms downstairs. LIPIA has
been trying to recruit more female instructors to change this,
but they are still outnumbered at least three to one as of 2019.
LIPIA also claims to have the largest library in all of Southeast
Asia today.

As one might expect, the books of Ibn Abd al-Wahhab have
always been a tentpole of LIPIA's curriculum. But the teaching
itself was never purely Wahhabi, and in the 1990s, LIPIA became
a hotbed of Muslim Brotherhood—oriented political Islamists,
as opposed to apolitical purist Salafis. That's why the university became a prime recruiting spot for the Prosperous Justice Party (PKS), Indonesia's most successful Islamist political
party. PKS recruited students from LIPIA and other universities in a highly organized manner that makes it unique in Indonesia, where party politics tend to coalesce around personalities
instead of ideas. Abshar-Abdalla once went on a rafting trip in
Bogor with LIPIA classmates that turned out to be a recruiting
event for Tarbiyah, the student wing of PKS.

Some of LIPIA's most influential alumni are members of
the modern PKS, including former party president Hidayat Nur

66   Wahid. Others include the hardline cleric Habib Rizieq Shihab, founder of the hardline Islamic Defenders Front that shaped the 2017 Jakarta election; the Salafi-jihadist Jafar Umar Thalib; and the popular Salafi preacher and radio preacher Yazid bin Abdul Qadir Jawas.

The LIPIA website entices applicants today with free tuition, a monthly allowance, "smooth" (*halus*) Arabic, opportunities to pursue graduate degrees in Saudi Arabia, free lecture books, and experienced lecturers from home and abroad. LIPIA graduates often go on to study in the affiliate university in Riyadh or at IUM. As of 2018, 2,230 Indonesians had graduated IUM since its founding. That seems high, but consider that far more than that number study in Egypt in a single year; for instance, in 2004, 3,528 Indonesian students were in Egypt, mostly at Al-Azhar. This makes the imprint of LIPIA alumni even more impressive.

The university receives far more applications than it can accept, because tuition and boarding are all free. So there is now even a backup plan for Indonesian students who want a Saudi education but don't get through LIPIA's competitive application process. Some Indonesians have sought an alternative course of study at Al-Madinah International University, or MEDIU, a Saudi-funded university based in Malaysia that offers online degree programs for any interested undergraduates and post-graduates, in both Arabic and English. MEDIU was founded in Medina in 2004 and relocated to Malaysia in 2007. Its financial backing and curriculum are both fully Saudi and it has become a valuable new path for Indonesians to attain a Gulf education. Which, given its reputation and influential alumni, is a completely understandable desire.

The Most Important Office in Jakarta

Indonesia's Saudi embassy is housed in a bland downtown sky-scraper on the Rasuna Said highway, but the religious attaché's office is in an elegant off-white mansion in the upscale residential neighborhood of Menteng. I met the last religious attaché, Saad Namase, in February 2018, when he was three months into his job. The religious attaché is a separate bureau within the Saudi embassy with a staff of about thirty people. The office is in charge of the proselytization activities of the embassy in Indonesia, often in heavy-handed and deeply personal ways. Abshar-Abdalla has called it the "most important office in Jakarta."

Namase was, like most Saudi officials in Indonesia, dressed in a flowing white *thobe* and checked headdress. I asked Namase, who spoke very softly and through a translator, what the office does in Indonesia.

"All we do is encourage Islam in Indonesia," he said, after some moments.

"Do you still fund mosques?"

"Perhaps. I'm not sure." He pled ignorance given his relatively recent arrival.

I never got to meet him again, because he was frequently home in Saudi Arabia. According to the 2016–17 report of the Saudi Dawa Ministry, which oversees the attaché's office, Indonesia was the site of 9,195 Saudi-sponsored lectures, 29,780 preaching sessions, and 5,153 tours. In 2013–14, the ministry noted 44 conversions to Islam in Indonesia due to its activities.

In May 2019, Namase made headlines for trying to bribe Indonesia's Religious Affairs Minister, Lukman Saifuddin. Namase had given him $35,000 in cash for holding a Quran

68   recitation competition, which Saifuddin did not report to the Corruption Eradication Commission. Shortly afterward, Namase was removed from his post, and it had not been filled again as of late 2019.

And his predecessor as religious attaché, Sheikh Ibrahim bin Sulaiman Alnughaimshi, was also implicated in the scandal, though his posting in Indonesia ended years ago. Alnughaimshi served in his post for sixteen years, from 2000 to 2016, and was a highly influential and active presence in Indonesia. Under his leadership, the attaché's office set up or endowed Islamic centers in places like Mentawai, the remote islands off the coast of Sumatra, and Sorong and Jayapura in Papua, the easternmost (and highly contested) province of Indonesia. They would partner with local Islamic organizations in these cities, recruit teachers and imams, buy land with Saudi support, and build Islamic centers, according to Dr. Shobahussurur, an Indonesian scholar who used to work for the attaché.

The attaché's office recruited promising young candidates through an exam, sort of like a civil service exam, and also assess them on their character and disposition. Then they were "ready to go anywhere" per Shobahussurur and were shipped out to conduct dawa in cities like Ambon and Medan, where they received monthly salaries for overseeing regional missionary activities like sending books to Islamic schools and setting up or funding mosques.

The Ivy League for Jihadists

Indonesia lost its innocence on October 12, 2002. It happened in Kuta—which means "town," but this was Bali's "town," so it was a tourist nerve center. October 12 was a Saturday, on the tail end of the Southern Hemisphere's summer, and loads of Australian tourists and sportspeople had decamped to Bali like migratory birds. Three bombs went off that night. The first, which exploded near the US consulate, was symbolic and killed nobody. Then, at 11:08 p.m., two loud cracks erupted simultaneously on opposite sides of the street. On one, a van detonated 1,500 pounds of explosives at the Sari nightclub, leaving a crater where it stalled on the street. The club's thatched roof went up in flames that rained down on its patrons, some of whom burned to death.

Across the street, a young man in white robes walked into an Irish bar called Paddy's Pub and blew himself up. The electronic music was drowned by screams. Soccer players on their first trips abroad watched their drinking buddies burn alive. In the parking lot, a Balinese ice cream truck driver's head was blown off while he was still in the vehicle, the ice cream jingle still chiming over the shrieking survivors.

That night, more than two hundred people died from the blasts and more than two hundred others were severely burned or injured. The island's morgue could barely handle so many corpses. The Balinese who lived there started to stream in within hours to place woven baskets of flower offerings on the street and by the ruined bar. No one had a frame of reference for such a tragedy. Although Indonesia is the world's largest Muslim-majority country, Salafi-jihadism like that which toppled the Twin Towers just a year earlier had yet to wash up on its shores in a major way. The Bali Bombings—masterminded by the Al Qaeda–affiliated jihadist group Jemaah Islamiyah—woke Indonesia to the terrorists who lived inside its borders.

After the bombings, whispers emerged about a so-called "Ivy League for jihadists," the Ngruki boarding school in Central

70   Java. Four of the Bali bombers were graduates: Mukhlas, Idris, Mubarok, and Amrozi, the "smiling assassin" who grinned at his prosecutors in a televised court testimony. The school actually opened three decades before the Bali Bombings, in 1972, with an endowment from the Saudi king Faisal.

Saudi fingerprints are all over the Salafi-jihadist networks of Indonesia and directly contributed to Indonesia's most traumatic terror attack ever. Was Ngruki a concerted Saudi effort to export Wahhabism or one among the hundreds of sundry projects that the kingdom financed in the years of peak dawa? The answer is somewhere in between.

The full name of the Ngruki school is Pondok Pesantren al-Mukmin; its cognomen comes from the suburb of Ngruki, outside Surakarta in Central Java, where it is located. The word *pondok*, which means "hut," turns out to be a misnomer. What you see when you approach the Ngruki school by road is the spiraling gold minaret of its massive campus mosque and then, through the iron gates, across a wide sandy courtyard, the boys' dormitory, a three-story cream-and-white edifice with "NGRUKI" emblazoned in white tiles on the roof. Fluttering banners around the campus exhort you to, "Learn Arabic, the Language of God." In the 1990s, they used to say, "Jihad is a Way of Life." About 1,500 students, both girls and boys, exit their prayers in unruly rows. Many of the teenage girls wear burqas, but the boys wear checkered sarongs and stiff white caps—in the traditional Javanese, not Salafi, style. The school has been somewhat mainstreamed and has been forced to adopt the national curriculum since coming under fire in 2002. But in the 1980s, Ngruki refused to even fly the Indonesian flag.

The so-called "Ngruki network" of jihadists was strongly
influenced and supported by Saudi Arabia. "It started with
Sungkar and Ba'asyir," said Nasir Abbas, a former Jemaah
Islamiyah jihadist and Afghan war guerrilla who turned over a
new leaf after jail and now works as a counterextremism advisor
to the Indonesian government.

He was referring to Abdullah Sungkar and Abu Bakar
Ba'asyir, the two key extremists who helped the Ngruki network coalesce in the 1970s and 1980s. They were both of Yemeni
Hadhrami descent. Like most of the prominent conservative
Muslim figures of their generation, Sungkar was well acquainted
with Mohammad Natsir, who made him the head of the Surakarta branch of DDII in 1970 and suggested that he build a school
there. The school was established in 1972 after Natsir arranged
an endowment from King Faisal. They built its campus in Ngruki
village. DDII enlisted many lecturers from LPBA, the precursor
to LIPIA university, to teach at Ngruki, including some teachers
from the Middle East. The Bali bombing project was plotted in
various forms starting in 1985 and sometimes was known by the
code phrase "studying the Arabic language."

At one point, Sungkar and Ba'asyir had to flee arrest in
Indonesia and went to Saudi Arabia on forged passports, where
they personally met the important Wahhabi cleric Bin Baz. The
sheikh counseled them that even the Prophet Muhammad faced
a period of exile and that they should wait out their exile in
Peshawar, from where they could easily join the Afghan jihad.

The Afghanistan conflict, heavily financed by both Saudi
Arabia and the US, to the tune of about $3 billion apiece, proved
to be extremely influential for extremism in Indonesia. The

72   cosmopolitan mujahideen brigades were a crucible for jihadists who would go on to wreak havoc in their far-flung home countries. Three of the Bali bombers were Afghanistan veterans.

"We Indonesians were not the best fighters," admitted Abbas, who now lives in South Jakarta. "We were a bit lazy." But the point of the jihad, as Sungkar told his cadres at the time, was not to fight the Soviet Union, but to learn how to wage jihad in Indonesia. The Indonesians were trained by Abdullah Azzam, the Saudi-backed Palestinian jihadist, and fought in the heavily Wahhabi unit.

After their Afghanistan stint, Sungkar and Ba'asyir finally had both the skills and manpower to start Jemaah Islamiyah (JI), a terrorist group that became the Southeast Asian branch of Al Qaeda, in 1993. JI set up more than twenty Salafi-jihadist schools across Indonesia and Malaysia. Nasir Abbas branched off to the Philippines, where he set up a terrorist training camp in Mindanao. Within a decade, they pulled off the long-awaited Bali bombing, and managed to execute even more bombings in its wake—at the Jakarta Marriott hotel in 2003, the Australian embassy in 2004, and even once more in Bali in 2005— until most of the key terrorists were finally rounded up or forced underground.

The Ngruki network was headquartered in Surakarta, but other influential Afghan alumni set up a base in Yogyakarta, the cultural heart of Central Java, perched on the edge of the Java Sea.

The most influential extremist from the Yogyakarta contingent was Jafar Umar Thalib, who rallied a Salafi-jihadist militia to fight Christians in the Moluccas in the early 2000s. Thalib was born in East Java in 1961 and studied briefly at LIPIA before finishing his studies in Pakistan. He fought in the Afghanistan jihad and returned to Indonesia after the fall of Suharto in 1998. In April 2000, he organized a gathering of ten thousand people at the Senayan stadium in Jakarta to encourage jihad in eastern Indonesia, where he warned of impending conflict between Christians and Muslims in the turmoil that followed the Suharto dictatorship's collapse.

On the basis of his support, Thalib created a ragtag militia called Laskar Jihad and led them into bloody communal battles around the city of Ambon for two years, from 2000 to 2002. At least nine thousand people were killed in that conflict. Hundreds of Christians were forcibly converted to Islam and some were even forcibly circumcised. The anti-Christian paranoia of Thalib recalls the nonviolent, but deeply felt, paranoia of Mohammad Natsir in the 1960s, so it's unsurprising Laskar Jihad's activities were supported by the humanitarian branch of DDII.

While all this was unfolding in the east, a nonviolent but puritanical Salafi movement was taking shape inside Yogyakarta. Chomsawa Safwan, known by his *nom du guerre* Abu Nida, fought alongside Jafar Umar Thalib in Afghanistan and briefly even taught him, but then broke with Thalib over his jihadist leanings. Abu Nida was more interested in and inspired by the systematic nature of Wahhabi dawa than its violent applications. After attending a DDII dawa course, he caught the attention of Mohammad Natsir, who recommended him for LIPIA, and he went on to study in Riyadh with a Muslim World League scholarship. He briefly taught at Ngruki school too. He developed a reputation as a charismatic preacher and set up Salafi study groups in at least a dozen cities in Java and Sulawesi. In 1992, he created a foundation called As-Sunnah in Yogyakarta to more

74   easily receive Gulf funds, both from Saudi Arabia and other Gulf countries like Kuwait. In 2000, he built a Salafi boarding school called the Islamic Center Bin Baz (ICBB), after the Saudi Wahhabi sheikh. Today, ICBB is the biggest Salafi institution in Yogyakarta, with 1,500 students from kindergarten through high school. As recently as 2015, the Saudi ambassador and former religious attaché actively attended events at ICBB, which was designated as a home for "Salafi youth."

Through Abu Nida's networks, Yogyakarta rapidly became a major center of Salafism in Indonesia. Abu Nida also started a Salafi magazine, also called *As-Sunnah,* which still to this day publishes religious opinions based on the work of Saudi scholars like Bin Baz. Abu Nida remains a senior Salafi figure, though intermittent years of crackdown have made him reclusive outside his preexisting base of acolytes. Now sixty-five, he has a long gray beard and occasionally blogs. His Salafi communities are large, but are closed off from greater Yogyakarta, whose easygoing residents bristle at their visible difference. In 2015, local residents refused to allow the ICBB school to expand its campus.

For much of the 2010s, it seemed like Salafi-jihadism in Indonesia was under control. With the major JI terrorists in jail, subsequent jihadists sublimated their radicalism into immigrating to Syria to join ISIS. Abdullah Sungkar died in 1999 and Abu Bakar Ba'asyir is eighty-one years old and still in jail. Jihadists actually started to backslide in skill: at least four suicide bombings from this decade in Indonesia ended up killing only the bomber.

Then Surabaya happened. Over the course of two days in May 2018, three different families bombed three churches and a police station in East Java, killing fifteen victims—and thirteen

attackers. The youngest bomber was an eight-year-old girl. The
bombings were planned by a deadly new jihadist group called
Jamaah Ansharut Daulah (JAD), which radicalized the Indonesian bombers through study groups where they discussed jihad
and watched videos of ISIS operations in Iraq and Syria.

JAD came together in 2015 as a secret meeting of thirty men
organized by Saiful Munthohir, an alumnus of the Laskar Jihad
militia in Poso, who all pledged allegiance to ISIS. JAD's spiritual
leader is Aman Abdurrahman, a Salafi-jihadist preacher who was
sentenced to jail in 2010 for an accessory role in the Bali bombings. Even from behind bars, he was the animating ideologue of
the group—he allegedly planned it before he was sentenced—and
he gave his blessing to the circle led by Munthohir. His sermons
circulated widely as cassettes. He was fluent in Arabic, memorized the Quran, and wrote a book on why Islam and democracy
are incompatible. He studied for seven years at LIPIA.

Aman was sentenced to death in 2018 for inspiring the Surabaya attacks. But his story, and the roles of alumni of Jafar Umar
Thalib's Salafi-jihadist militia, perfectly shows the infinitely
long half-life of the jihadist infrastructure constructed by Saudi
institutions, Saudi alumni, and Saudi ideas in Indonesia. Not
only did Aman study at LIPIA for seven years, but he went on to
lecture there for a year after his graduation in 1999. One won-
ders what the future holds for his former students.

The Intolerance Factory

The imprint of Salafi-jihadism on Indonesia has been undoubtedly tragic, but in terms of sheer numbers of people involved, relatively small. Perhaps the greater absolute legacy of Saudi dawa has been the rise of virulent religious intolerance, both against religious minorities, like Christians, and against Muslims who are considered to be "deviant," like the Shia and Ahmadiyya. The persecution of non-Sunni Muslims has been central to Saudi state-sanctioned religion and foreign policy. Wahhabism centers on prosecuting other Muslims as not Muslim enough or not Muslims at all.

Saudi Arabia has supported a staggering number of actors in Indonesia in this regard, from solitary ideologues to populist Islamist groups.

One of the strangest is Amin Djamaluddin, a one-man conspiracy factory who lives in Jakarta. Djamaluddin runs—and *is,* because he is its only real employee—a think tank vaguely called Lembaga Penelitian dan Pengkajian Islam (LPPI), the "Institute for Islamic Study and Research." Through LPPI, he has published seventeen books criticizing different minority groups: the Shia, the Ahmadiyya, an upstart movement called Gafatar, the Haqqaniyya Sufi order, and indigenous Javanese religions known as *kebatinan*. Djamaluddin's office in Cikini, Central Jakarta, was purchased for him by a Saudi businessman in 2002, whose name he claims to have forgotten, but which was arranged by DDII. LPPI has also been funded directly by DDII since its creation in 1985. Its motto is simple: "To eradicate deviant sects."

Djamaluddin, now in his seventies, is small, with thick eyebrows and a stiff beard. He walked into his office in Central Jakarta holding a messenger bag screen-printed with a logo that commemorated a protest against Ahmadiyya Muslims that he had helped organize in 2005. Over the course of our meeting, he pulled out various supporting materials from this bag: crumbling clippings from his old newspaper columns criticizing liberal Islamic intellectuals, which first brought him to Mohammad Natsir's attention in the 1980s; the polemic books that he has written over the years; photos from the seminar he once organized to debate whether Shia Muslims should be allowed to exist in Indonesia.

Djamaluddin thinks there's an undue focus on pluralism in modern Indonesia, whose national motto is "Unity in Diversity." "Pluralism does not mean you should include people who counter Islam," he told me. Though he is eccentric, his arguments have the ear of several politicians. In West Nusa Tenggara province, he held a seminar for the governor explaining why the Ahmadiyya are heretics, and the governor promptly forwarded his memo to all the schools in the region, so that they could be vigilant against "deviant" students.

78   The Ahmadiyya are a tiny minority in Indonesia: estimates range from 50,000 to 400,000, in a country of over 260 million. They follow a nineteenth-century revivalist Islamic movement that was started in British India by a man called Mirza Ghulam Ahmad (1835–1908), who claimed to be the Messiah expected to appear in end times, according to Islamic eschatology. Many Muslims consider the Ahmadiyya to be heterodox to the point of blasphemy, and they are persecuted worldwide. In Indonesia, this persecution has been greatly intensified by Saudi dawa.

The first anti-Ahmadiyya fatwa in Indonesia was issued in 1980, soon after the Muslim World League's declaration, in 1974, that Ahmadiyya were a deviant sect. A second wave of violence gripped the island of Lombok from 1999 to 2005, starting when an Ahmadi man there was murdered, and ending with hundreds of Ahmadiyya being driven from their homes into refugee camps, where they remain today. Djamaluddin helped organize these mob actions and has proudly framed news articles from these events in his office. The Indonesian Muslim Clerics Council issued another national anti-Ahmadiyya fatwa in 2005. In 2011, a mob of 1,500 attacked an Ahmadiyya site in West Java and killed three people. Djamaluddin was involved in this, too, and even threatened "unrest" to the provincial government if they allowed the Ahmadiyya to organize counterprotests there.

Djamaluddin should be a fringe figure. He is an unhinged ideologue whose seventeen books are repetitive in their themes and loose in their analysis. They are typically a collage of polemic and news clippings, plus first-person anecdotes and letters from people who write to him about their deviant neighbors from all across Indonesia. Their titles are things like *Ahmadiyya and the Hijacking of the Quran* and *Beware the Shia Movement in*

Indonesia. And yet, his agenda has been mainstreamed by the
religious establishment and has led to deadly violence.

The anti-Shia campaign in Indonesia has been just as virulent and also bears a distinct Saudi fingerprint. The Sunni-Shia
opposition was not crystallized in Indonesia until the late twentieth century, when Saudi dawa began there in earnest. Distinctly
Shia practices like celebrating the mourning month of Muharram
were commonplace in Aceh and South Sumatra for several centuries; people who partook in these rituals would not have called
themselves Shiites per se but just Muslims. But today, Indonesia
actually has a dedicated National Anti-Shia Alliance.

Demonizing Shiism became central to Saudi discourse after
1979 and was amplified in Indonesia through DDII and its *Media
Dakwah* magazine. In 1997, Amin Djamaluddin organized the
influential national seminar on Shiism in Indonesia at Jakarta's
Istiqlal Mosque, which lay the groundwork for state-sanctioned
anti-Shia violence in the following years.

In 2006, a Sunni mob disrupted a Shia celebration of Ashura
in East Java; in 2007, there was a thousand-person anti-Shia
protest in the same province; from 2007–2010, a Shia boarding
school near Jakarta was consistently vandalized and stoned;
mob violence drove out a Shia community from Madura Island
in 2011.

"Frankly, it's gotten so much worse in the last decade," said
Jalaluddin Rahmat, one of Indonesia's most prominent Shiites,
now a Member of Parliament from Bandung, a city about three
hours east of Jakarta. I met him in his home before the votes had
been counted in the 2019 national election. "Even though they
were trying so hard to seed an anti-Shia campaign in the 1980s, it
didn't take root until much later," he said. Rahmat is a thoughtful

80   intellectual who tends to hunch over during conversation, with his elbows on his knees, as if not to take up too much space. Once a self-described "soft Salafi," he converted to Shiism in the wake of the Iranian Revolution, when he was one of the many Indonesian intellectuals invited to Tehran. For him, Shiism is the "religion of the oppressed" and it aligned with his burgeoning Marxist beliefs. He created a publishing house called Al-Mizan to translate Iranian books and was instrumental to creating Shia study groups in the university campuses of Bandung.

He is Indonesia's only openly Shia lawmaker, though he intimated that there are others. Unfortunately, his constituency of Bandung is also home to the National Anti-Shia Alliance, known by its Indonesian acronym of ANNAS. What's most interesting about ANNAS is that it's not a Saudi project, and it actually distances itself from the kingdom today, even though its rhetoric was clearly seeded by Saudi dawa of the 1980s and 1990s.

"When we talk about anti-Shia, it does not necessarily mean we have connection with Saudi Arabia," said Atip Latipulhayat, a law professor—somewhat ironically, of human rights law—at Padjadaran University in Bandung. "That's bullshit." Atip described his background as decidedly Indonesian; he comes from a family involved in PERSIS, one of the homegrown Islamist movements of the early twentieth century. As if to underscore the point, he wore batik, the traditional wax-patterned Indonesian fabric; kept an Indonesian flag on his desk; and left his pinky finger inked to prove that he had voted in the recent election.

It does no favors for ANNAS to tie itself to the Gulf today, because one of their major points is that Shiism is a nefarious foreign invasion into Indonesia. "Shiism everywhere is political," he claimed. "It's impossible to talk about the Shia without talking about Iran. . . . Have you seen the Iranian constitution? It states that the government has a responsibility to disseminate Shiism. That's a problem for ANNAS."

ANNAS has at least thirty members in Bandung and fifteen outposts in other cities, said Atip. They are building a brick-and-mortar headquarters soon, with donations from the local Muslim community. For now, they meet at a mosque in Bandung. When I asked him how Shia dawa operates in Indonesia, he was vague: well, it's not through conversions per se, but Shia "influence," he said. What are the signs of someone becoming Shia? I asked him. "Well, it's very legalistic . . . and it disrupts the unified Islamic creed in Indonesia," he said, not clarifying much.

"And!" he remembered, a few minutes later. "They never properly recognize the *Rashidun,*" the first four "rightly guided" caliphs. (The major point of divergence between Sunnis and Shiites is the former believe that the first caliph, Abu Bakr, who was appointed by the Prophet Muhammad, was his rightful successor, whereas the latter believe in the familial line of succession through the Prophet's son-in-law, Ali.) "They must return back to the straight path," he said, with finality. He did not endorse the violent acts perpetrated on Indonesian Shia, but held firm that they simply do not have a place in the country.

What ANNAS shows is that, within thirty years, Saudi Arabia's anti-Shia propaganda in Indonesia was so effective as to have become redundant. Thus, even if material Saudi donations slow to a trickle, Saudi ideas will still have definitively shaped the religious climate of modern Indonesia, where the list of victims of Sunni majoritarianism grows by the day. Saudi dawa's cumulative efforts have ensured that ideas like Salafism and anti-Shiism have a popular audience now. Every Saudi

official could leave Indonesia tomorrow and there would still be
a vibrant Salafi ecosystem in place.

Salafi Enclaves

Indonesian Salafis grew into their identities after 9/11, when
much of the active Saudi funding around the world dried up.
Its pure Salafi communities today are characterized by a certain
inward looking—ness: their communities are closed, insular,
dressed differently. For Salafis, their clothing and lifestyle
choices are an expression of their belief that society should be
gradually Islamized and that they can lead by example.

They are not extravagantly well funded. For instance, in Yogyakarta, there is the thriving Salafi community overseen by the
aforementioned cleric Abu Nida, who was supported in the '80s
and '90s by Saudi Arabia, as well as Kuwait and Yemen. But the
modern Salafi networks of Yogyakarta have taken to the new millennium largely through grassroots and low-cost initiatives.
The Yogyakarta-based Salafi radio station RadioMuslim gets
small donations from its listeners, including many who set up
a monthly direct debit of IDR 50,000 (about $3); just from such
donations, their monthly budget has increased from eight million rupiah in 2011 to thirty-eight million rupiah in 2018. And
there are dozens of other Indonesian Salafi magazines, websites,
and YouTube personalities. In Jakarta, the Medina alumnus and
prominent Salafi preacher Bachtiar Natsir gives several popular
lectures a week at his mosque in Tebet. On Sundays, they include
special classes for women on how to be a good Islamic wife.

The Saudi Dawa Ministry's material support of the Indonesian religious attaché has decreased over the last five years,
according to its own reports. The Philippines is now its biggest

target in Southeast Asia, receiving three times as many printed
materials as Indonesia. (This may be due in part to Saudi aid
to the Muslim-majority Southern Philippines after its jihadist
insurgency in 2017.) But Indonesian institutions have adjusted.
Once DDII's Gulf funding dried up, it was replaced in part by
politicians like the evergreen presidential loser Prabowo, a military general turned cabinet minister, who personally funded
DDII throughout the 2000s.

Another example of a regional Salafi ecosystem, to look
outside Java, is in Batam, a rather seedy resort island in a special duty-free economic zone, just across the bay from Singapore. That there are Salafis here at all is remarkable, and is in
itself a testament to Saudi dawa. Batam has little to recommend
it tax-free shopping and cheap bars, but in the last ten years, it
has also become home to a prominent Salafi radio station called
Hang Radio and multiple Salafi boarding schools. I visited
one of the schools, Pesantren Anshur al-Sunnah, in Batam's
main Salafi neighborhood of Cendana. The school's director,
an Acehnese man and Medina graduate named Wildan, agreed
to speak to me, but only through a partitioned room, because
he could not spend time in the presence of a woman who was
not related to him. He passed me a brochure about the school
through a small square aperture in the drywall. The facilities are
bare-bones, but it educates over 150 students from Indonesia,
Malaysia, and Singapore.

In Batam's busy downtown, Hang Radio runs an impressive office and recording studio. The station is decades old but it
took a religious turn only in 2004 when its owner, a local businessman named Zein Alatas, became a Salafi in a fit of mid-
life piety. Now, it broadcasts twenty straight hours of religious

84 content every day, including sermons by visiting clerics, and Batam has become a crossroads for Salafis in Southeast Asia. The island made headlines in 2016 when it rejected 418 passport applications from Batam residents who were suspected of intent to join ISIS, and Hang Radio was cited by local authorities as a key factor behind the convicts' increasingly radical views.

It seems likely that there will be a few more Indonesian Salafi enclaves like the one in Batam in the near future, but they will no longer be direct products of Saudi dawa. Batam is a great example of the transition from Saudi-fomented Salafism to site-specific networks, because its Salafi nodes include both a Medina alumnus and a wealthy Indonesian who was drawn to the ideology on his own terms, without studying it formally. There was no internet when Mohammad Natsir first brought Saudi dawa to Indonesia, but with the advent of globalization, anyone can become a Salafi.

Saudi dawa is not irresistible. The largest population of Indonesians in the Gulf is neither scholarship students nor clerics, but migrant workers, of whom there have been over one million per year in recent years. Many of them are poor women from rural areas or outer provinces, and a significant number have been horrifically abused physically, emotionally, or sexually. If Saudi Arabia was some kind of magically compelling religious climate, many more of these women would become Salafis. Instead, the exact opposite sometimes happens.

At the Iranian Cultural Center in Jakarta, during the Shia celebration of Muharram in 2018, I met a woman whose experience as a maid in Jeddah was so awful that she literally converted to Shiism in complete rejection of Saudi Arabia's puritanical Sunni traditions. This admixture of "rejection and admiration"

of Saudi Arabia by its migrant workers often produces the exact
opposite result of Saudi dawa, as Laurent Bonnefoy has also
observed of migrant workers from Yemen.

Although Saudi dawa is decreasing in absolute terms and
Indonesian Salafis are standing on their own feet, one cultural
factor that still enshrines the Saudi brand in Indonesia is the
uneasy inferiority complex held by many Southeast Asian Muslims. Despite the great numerical advantage of Indonesia's
Muslims—there are more Muslims in the archipelago than in
all the Gulf states combined—ideas rarely flow in the opposite
direction. Indonesia's traditional Muslim establishment has
periodically tried to project its brand of "Islam Nusantara," or
"Archipelago Islam," on the world stage, but it remains ideologically muddled. And it offers little to contest the authoritative,
straightforward texts of the Wahhabi canon. Islam Nusantara
theoretically stands for tolerance, but its acolytes are often just
as intolerant of Shia and Ahmadiyya as Salafis. And while Islam
Nusantara is theoretically accepting of Java's Hindu-Buddhist
past, it gets lost in the specifics of how and why, because it's
hard to argue why those rituals don't constitute "polytheism" in
a debate whose terms are now set by Wahhabis.

Thus, the image of Saudi Arabia remains strong in both the
religious and nonreligious spheres. Indonesian Salafi clerics
nearly always cite Saudi scholars in their rulings and nearly all
ordinary Muslims save up to visit Mecca and Medina. Within
Indonesia's thriving Islamic-capitalist consumer economy,
products depicting Mecca's Kaaba shrine, from clocks to cal-
endars, are ubiquitous. I once bought iced tea from a woman in
Manado, in North Sulawesi, whose hijab was simply embroi-
dered with the word "Saudi" in cursive script: the kingdom as

86   brand and logo. Several grocery stores in Jakarta sell "Saudi Choice" cotton swabs, which are advertised as "the principle-based choice."

From Aceh to Papua

Indonesia's variant of "from sea to shining sea" is the phrase "from Aceh to Papua," which denotes the sweep of the archipelago, from the ultra-conservative former sultanate of Aceh, on the rim of the Bay of Bengal, to Papua, the misty Indonesian half of New Guinea, home to hundreds of mostly Melanesian ethnic groups and very controversially a part of Indonesia at all. Aceh is the only province in Indonesia that has been allowed to implement sharia, which was a concession granted in 2005 when it signed a peace treaty after a long separatist rebellion. These days, Aceh usually makes the news for sensational reasons like the public floggings it levies on sodomites and adulterers. Meanwhile, Papua is extremely underdeveloped, almost forbidden to journalists, and mostly Christian, due to Dutch missionary activity. Which province would you guess is more influenced by Saudi dawa today?

If you guessed Aceh, that's exactly wrong. Aceh certainly *received* Saudi charity after its extreme devastation in the 2004 Indian Ocean tsunami, when over 160,000 people in the province died or went missing. The Saudi Charity Campaign promptly set up in the provincial capital of Banda Aceh and donated more than $45 million, which included two orphanages, almost five hundred new houses, a hospital, and restoration of the main Baiturrahman Mosque. In 2007, it also opened a local branch of LIPIA to teach Arabic to about two hundred students. Salafi study groups started popping up at mosques around the province.

What you might expect is that the people of Aceh, which styles itself as the "Veranda to Mecca" and proudly claims to be the first place in Indonesia where people converted to Islam, slowly became Saudi-oriented Salafis. But the opposite happened: Aceh accepted Saudi aid but drew a hard line at the proselytization that typically accompanies Saudi charity.

This wasn't just a theoretical pushback but also a physical one. In 2007, Acehnese villagers burned down the Ma'had As Sunnah school in the town of Lampeuneurut, which was started by a Saudi-educated Javanese teacher. In 2013, traditional Acehnese clerics challenged a leading Salafi preacher to a public debate, which he declined, likely out of fear. In March 2016, locals attacked another Salafi school in Lam Awe and all the students had to evacuate. Most striking was the physical confrontation between Salafis and traditionalists in the Saudi-refurbished Baiturrahman Mosque. Acehnese ulama occupied the mosque during Friday prayers in June 2015 and forced the Salafi imam there to lead rites in their traditional style, rather than in a perceived "Wahhabi" style. At issue were mainly rituals: the traditional clerics wanted the imam to hold a staff during his sermon and for the call to prayer to be sung twice, instead of just once. But the clash put a face to the brewing resistance among Acehnese citizens, who resented being taken advantage of spiritually after their traumatic natural disaster.

Banda Aceh today has been handsomely reconstructed and is one of the best-developed regional capitals in the country. The Acehnese continue traditions like celebrating Maulid, the

Prophet's birthday, which is hated by Wahhabis. There is still stringent sharia that polices Christians, improperly veiled women, and transgender and queer people. But that sharia is not a Saudi import; it is distinctly Acehnese. The Banda Aceh branch of LIPIA, which was once intended to become a fully operating university campus, has contented itself with staying as an Arabic language institute.

Aceh shows how Saudi charity is neither a done deal nor a one-way street. Aceh may have been a special case because of its uniquely assertive regional identity; even in the 1980s, the Free Aceh Movement, which trained in Libya, refused to send members to Saudi Arabia out of a distaste for Wahhabi doctrine. And Salafis have not left Aceh altogether, so clashes may well break out again. But not without resistance.

Meanwhile, Papua has been the site of a guerrilla insurgency since 1963 against the Indonesian military, and over 100,000 people have died in their clash to date. Much of Papua is covered in rain forest and its peopled towns are sometimes separated by hundreds of miles, which is one reason for its cultural diversity. It's a difficult area to work in, with even more bureaucratic red tape than in the rest of Indonesia. You couldn't design a harder place for an outside actor to penetrate.

And yet: Jafar Umar Thalib was there. The infamous Salafi-jihadist, former LIPIA student, and founder of the Laskar Jihad militia has a new project, and it's called "Papua Dakwah," preaching in Papua. Since 2015, the self-professed Wahhabi has been setting up Islamic boarding schools across the contested province. So far he has already built the Ihya'as Sunnah Islamic Boarding School in Keerom Regency and another in the city of Jayapura, and he has plans to build two more in the cities

of Tolikara and Sorong. His followers in Jayapura have clashed
with local Christians and there have been a number of protests
against his presence there, but since the Papua branch of the
Indonesia Muslim Clerics Council has not pushed him out, they
are largely powerless.

Papuans say the Papua Dakwah movement is part of a more
insidious Indonesian strategy to incorporate Papua into the
country, by not merely occupying it, and by not merely ship-
ping thousands of Indonesians from other islands to work there
through its "transmigration" program, but also by converting
Papuans themselves to Islam. "Islamization is the only way to
control Papua," said Reverend Dora Balubun, a female priest at
the Injili Christian Church and representative of the Indonesian
Church Council (GKI) in Papua.

Under the mantle of Papua Dakwah, the proprietors of
Islamic boarding schools in Java have also been filling their
schools with Papuan children, many of whom are from Christian families. In Papuan cities like Bintuni, Wamena, Sorong,
and Asmat, preachers associated with a nonprofit called AFKN
Nuu War recruit parents and families to send their children
to Java, said Balubun. "We call it human trafficking," she said,
plainly. "Nuu War" comes from a Papuan dialect and means "the
land that keeps secrets."

Since 2000, AFKN has sent over 200 Muslim missionaries into Papua. As of July 2014, the group has circumcised
over 7,500 children in Wamena, Agats, Bintuni, and Keerom. It
also runs an Islamic boarding school called Pesantren Nuu War
in Bekasi, on the outskirts of the Jakarta metropolitan area. I
tried to visit the school in 2018 and was forcibly escorted out by
armed guards. Someone who was more welcome there was the

90   last Saudi Arabian ambassador, Osama Al Shuaibi. The Saudi embassy in Jakarta funded the brand-new mosque at the school and endorsed the proselytization of Ustad Fazlan, the leader of AFKN. In January 2018, the ambassador promised sixty new scholarships to LIPIA for Nuu War students and said that, in the last few years, sixty-three of them had already gotten places to study at LIPIA Jakarta and LIPIA Aceh, fully subsidized by the Saudi government.

"Arabic is the language of the Quran, so it is very important that candidates of Papuan origin . . . master the Arabic language, to improve the quality of the Papua dawa in the future," said the ambassador, speaking at the school in March 2017. Ustad Fadlan of AFKN Nuu War has also made several appearances at the Saudi Religious Attaché's office, according to social media posts from there.

Even though the scale of Saudi investments in Indonesia has decreased in absolute terms, they still know how to hit a target: by supporting Papua Dakwah, Saudi money is facilitating one of the most troubling religious developments in Indonesia today. And it's unsurprising that one of Indonesia's foremost Wahhabis and Saudi university alumni, Jafar Umar Thalib, is leading the charge on the ground. From Aceh to Papua, Saudi dawa is down but not out.

Nigeria's Salafi Ouroboros

Thirty-two-year-old Abdullahi Muhammad Musa was going up to celebrate Quds Day, the international day of solidarity with Palestine, in Nigeria's northern state of Zaria, in December 2015. He crammed into a sedan with six relatives in the capital city of Abuja and set off on the five-hour drive. Only he would come back alive.

All the others in that car, and at least 390 other people, were gunned down by the Nigerian military in what is now known as the Zaria Massacre. All were followers of the Islamic Movement in Nigeria, an outspoken Shia group that has long been under fire by Sunnis, Salafis, and the state. Like in many other parts of the Muslim world, including Indonesia, this anti-Shia sentiment was fueled in large part by Saudi-oriented Salafis. In Nigeria, it's taken a uniquely deadly turn.

The sectarian conflict is just one way in which Saudi dawa has changed Nigeria's religious landscape in the last half-century. Nigeria has the largest Muslim population in Africa.

92 It's estimated that roughly half of the country's 191 million people are Muslim, although religious demographics are so contentious that it has not been a question on the census since 1963. The country is a huge arena for global contests over Islamic dogma, just like Indonesia is in Southeast Asia. In such a volatile religious climate, the rise of Saudi-affiliated Salafism has created a great churn.

Saudi Arabia started its outreach to West Africa in the 1960s, shortly after Nigeria won independence from British rule in 1960. In what can now be considered a pattern, having just considered the scope of Saudi impact in Indonesia, King Faisal's administration partnered with several key Muslim leaders in Nigeria, many of whom were able to study in Medina and others of whom operated branches of transnational Saudi charities like the Muslim World League. Within a decade, a generation of Salafis emerged in northern Nigeria, whose Muslims had, until then, been predominantly Sufi or nondenominational. Salafis created the Izala movement for "preserving virtue" and were influential in deciding the shape of sharia, which was implemented across the Muslim north starting in 1999.

The most infamous Nigerians to identify as Salafis were members of Boko Haram, the Salafi-jihadist terrorist group responsible for hundreds of terror attacks and the kidnapping of thousands of schoolchildren since 2009. Boko Haram overtook ISIS as the world's deadliest terror group in 2015. But it did not emerge in a vacuum. The founder of Boko Haram studied with the most prominent Saudi-educated Salafi in Nigeria, Jafar Mahmud Adam, and even briefly sought refuge, like many Islamists under fire, in Saudi Arabia itself. And the Salafi-jihadism

of Boko Haram, although an anomaly, still emerged from the
rich Salafi tapestry that was knitted in Nigeria over the previous
half-century.

Saudi outreach encouraged the growth of Salafism in Nigeria
by strategically cultivating deep personal contacts in the postcolonial nation and seeding opportunities to study in the kingdom.
The resulting Salafis have clashed with both the reigning Sufi
orders and the parallel, Iran-affiliated Shia movement, but have
also been mainstreamed into government positions, and finally,
have laid the ideological groundwork for Boko Haram.

Over the Walls of Kano

The first Muslim immigration in history was to Africa, when
the persecuted Muslims of Mecca sought refuge in Ethiopia. In
1324, Mansa Musa, the fabulously rich king of Timbuktu, took
an epic pilgrimage to Mecca and spent so much gold along the
way that he deflated gold prices along his route for years. In the
nineteenth and twentieth centuries, West African scholars,
including those from present-day Nigeria, helped consolidate
the House of Saud's Wahhabi campaign within Saudi Arabia by
preaching the Wahhabi message to Bedouin tribes in rural areas.
Which is to say, there has been a rich two-way relationship
spanning centuries between the Gulf and sub-Saharan Africa.

When Saudi Arabia began its serious twentieth-century
dawa in Nigeria, the country was in tense postcolonial straits.
For one thing, it contained a diametrically opposed Muslim-
majority north and a Christian-majority south. This is not
unusual among modern African countries, which were traditionally organized on a horizontal axis before colonial rule

94   mixed them up across boundaries. (Muslim-majority Sudan
        and now-independent Christian-majority South Sudan is
        another example, as well as modern-day Chad.)

        Saudi dawa concentrated in Nigeria's north. The northern
        Muslim states have been administered by sharia since 2000,
        but they were a Muslim stronghold long before that. They are
        also, on the whole, less-developed on most vectors, including
        literacy, vaccination, and maternal mortality rates. The largest
        northern city is Kano, an ancient trade center in the Sahel, the
        wide semi-arid band that crosses Africa right below the Sahara
        Desert. In the heart of Kano is a walled old city of sand-colored
        mud houses, farm animals, open markets, and date palms. Out-
        side the ring road are the bustling offices and cheaply built
        homes of a growing metropolis. In the hot and dry months, a
        fine layer of dust and Sahel sand settles on every surface.

        There were Muslims in Kano as early as the fourteenth cen-
        tury, but Islam in northern Nigeria was consolidated with the
        nineteenth-century Sokoto jihad, in which a militant reformist
        scholar named Usman dan Fodio created a powerful caliphate
        of ten million people. The Sokoto Caliphate lasted for a century
        until it caved to British rule in 1903, and it was one of the most
        successful African polities in modern history. It also exempli-
        fied a regional tendency toward periodic, violent, intra-Muslim
        conflict.

        About 65 percent of Nigerian Muslims identify as Sufis, and
        northern Nigeria is home to two major Sufi brotherhoods: the
        Tijaniyya, who are localized in West Africa, and the Qadiriyya,
        a global order that originated in modern-day Iran. Although
        Sufism is typically depicted in the West with an emphasis on
        its mystical and transcendental elements, Sufi orders in this

region have at times been both political and violent. Sufism—
which is not a sect like Sunnah and Shia but an approach to
Islam, although the majority of Sufis are Sunnis—does place a
high value on a personal engagement with God and has developed distinctive practices, like ritual chanting and whirling, to
facilitate this. But Usman dan Fodio of the Sokoto Caliphate
was a Sufi too. (He was also a contemporary of Muhammad ibn
Abd al-Wahhab and was thus part of a remarkable nineteenth-
century efflorescence of puritanical movements in the Muslim
world, which also included the Padri Wars of Indonesia's ear-
liest Wahhabis.) Still, by the mid-twentieth century, the two
major Sufi orders had consolidated their power structures and
more or less peacefully coexisted in northern Nigeria.

Programmatic Saudi dawa in Nigeria started under the reign
of King Faisal, who pioneered the use of "Islamic solidarity"
(al-tadamun al-Islami) as a principle of Saudi foreign policy.
Sub-Saharan Africa was an attractive target because Communist movements were not very strong in most of the region, so
the Saudis were not fighting an uphill battle of ideas there as
they were in North Africa.

The very first international recruitment tour delegation
from the International University of Medina went to East Africa
in 1964 and the second went to West Africa in 1965. There
was a Nigerian who went on both of these tours, a remarkable
figure born and brought up in Medina named Umar Fallata. He
was one of those who helped preach Wahhabiyya to Saudi Bedouins and he eventually became the first secretary-general of
the Islamic University of Medina in 1962. Nigeria was identified as an important potential partner for Saudi Arabia, both
because of its size and its history with the Sokoto Caliphate. In

96   these early tours, IUM delegates downplayed Wahhabism per se, especially its anti-Sufi rhetoric, so as not to not offend local sensibilities. The delegation recommended giving material support to two key figures in the north: Ahmadu Bello, the first (and only) premier of the Northern Region, and Abubakar Gumi, a young scholar who had worked in Jeddah for several years as a hajj officer and had recently returned to Nigeria to lead a revivalist group called Jama'atu Nasril Islam (JNI), the Society for the Support of Islam. He was also serving Bello as the region's grand *qadi,* or judge.

Gumi would do for Nigeria what Mohammad Natsir did for Indonesia. He was a close friend and frequent visitor to the kingdom, a conduit and eyes on the ground for the dawa apparatus, and the intellectual locomotive behind the institutions that would shape the ideological landscape of the country. In 1988, he was awarded a King Faisal award by the kingdom, and he died in 1992 at age sixty-nine. By then, he had done more to connect Nigerian Islam with the Gulf than anyone else.

After the 1965 tour from IUM, the kingdom formed a plan to cultivate and spread scholarships through the key figures identified by the delegation, and then wait and see what happened next.

Commanding Virtue

As the first IUM tour trekked through Africa, King Faisal was still Prince Faisal, but he ascended to the throne later that year and personally befriended Premier Bello. From 1962 to 1965, Faisal gave 100,000 pounds a year to Bello to promote proselytization, which he promptly channeled in turn to Gumi. He used the funds to lead a vigorous conversion campaign across

Nigeria. Bello loved visiting Saudi Arabia, and between 1955 and 1965, he made pilgrimages at least twice a year, usually with Gumi in tow.

Communism may not have been such a strong threat in mid-century Nigeria, but Nasserism and Arab Socialism certainly were. After the 1952 Egyptian Revolution, Gamel Abdel Nasser made a strong push for pan-Islamic credentials in sub-Saharan Africa. He built schools for, sent cultural envoys to, and offered scholarships at Cairo's Al-Azhar specifically for black Africans.

In the 1960s, Gumi set up Nigerian operations of the Muslim World League, which didn't have a brick-and-mortar office but basically dispensed funds wherever he saw fit. In 1966, Premier Bello was killed in a violent military coup—the first of eight that would rock the country until 1999. This actually strengthened Gumi's position because the next military governor gave him even more leverage and free media access. Gumi used his platform to attack Sufis more vociferously, using open-air sermons, radio, television, and cassette tapes that are still circulated in Kano markets today. He preached across the region that no Muslim should accept a non-Muslim leader.

Not content with the scope of JNI, Gumi created another group in 1978, through his protégé Ismail Idris, called the Society of Removal of Innovation and Re-establishment of the Sunnah (Traditions of the Prophet). Even in Hausa, it's a mouthful: Jama'at Izalatul Bid'a wa Iqamatis Sunnah, or Izala for short. Izala is still influential today and its formation cemented the conservative turn in northern Nigeria, one that would climax in sharia and overripen into Salafi-jihadism. Although Izala was always led by and staffed by Nigerians, its agenda had every mark of the Wahhabi mission. It was founded to eradicate Sufi

98 practices, so-called polytheism (shirk), and unnecessary innovations (bidah) from Nigerian Islam.

Dr. Gumi, along with Idris, staked out Izala's home in Jos,
in Plateau State, at the heart of Nigeria's "Middle Belt" between
the Muslim North and Christian South. Idris worked locally
while Gumi traveled back and forth to Mecca.

Izala preachers were energetic and straightforward. They
relied on Ibn Abd al-Wahhab's *Book of Tawhid*, the key text of
Wahhabism, but spoke in demotic Hausa. Izala attacked various
local religious practices like visiting graves, carrying charms,
using holy water, divination, claiming to see Allah in dreams
and visions, and the veneration of Sufi saints. Its preachers even
discouraged eating meat slaughtered by Sufis.

The movement got a boost from demographic trends:
Nigeria was becoming more urban, more literate, and more
individualized in the 1970s after its own oil boom in 1973.
These new middle-class Nigerians were the perfect candidates for a movement that encouraged reading texts for
yourself instead of listening to traditional authorities. Izala's preaching sessions mushroomed. There were seven hundred nationwide sessions between 1978 and 1988, which were
recorded and amplified through radio and cassettes, and thousands more were held locally.

Izala members were systematic about building physical
mosques and schools dedicated to their ideology, which helped
the upstart movement make rapid grassroots gains against the
Sufi establishment. They often built mosques without both-
ering to get permission from the Emir of Kano, the state's hereditary spiritual leader, who is traditionally a Sufi. Up until 1900,

there was only one mosque in all of central Kano, but after 1978, Izala built hundreds of new ones, mostly outside the old city's walls. And more and more people in the burgeoning metropolis were moving to the periphery and the suburbs, as in any big city. Izala felt that the Emir and the Sufis could have the old city, with its sprawling markets and grand clay palace; the battle for hearts and minds could be fought elsewhere.

Due to their rapid and visible expansion, it became a self-perpetuating credo that Salafis had more money and more access to money than the traditional, languishing Sufi orders. Some people joined Izala in hopes of gaining a channel to Saudi financiers through Gumi, and he did help at least one businessman who joined the movement to get a major petroleum contract.

The new Salafis were combative in person too. They sparred constantly with Sufis in their first three years; Gumi gave popular sermons in Kaduna saying that anyone who recited a Tijaniyya prayer was an "unbeliever" and could be killed and were often harassed by authorities. Shaykh Abdullahi Garangamawa, a Medina graduate who now preaches in Kano, recalls being regularly detained in the 1980s. "People said we were bringing a 'new religion,'" he said, "because they didn't know what real Islam was." He was detained ten times by police and briefly held in jail twice in the early Izala years. But then he went to IUM to study sharia from 1991–1996 and said that, when he came back, "Izala had gone mainstream."

Not only had Izala gone mainstream during those short years, but it had also refocused its efforts from anti-Sufi screeds into promoting the implementation of sharia, which suddenly seemed like a real possibility in democratic Nigeria. They

100 shifted from inter-Muslim rivalry to a pan-Islamic goal. In a short time, Izala preachers became legitimate and mainstream, which meant they could play a huge role in deciding what sharia looked like. They were basically Salafis, but they nominally upheld the local Maliki school of jurisprudence common to West Africa, so their inputs could not be questioned too deeply. And sharia implementation reified one of their big ideas: to Islamize daily life.

There were many factors behind the sharia implementation process, which started in Zamfara State in 2000 and quickly spread to a dozen northern states including Kano. The majority of Muslim northerners supported it as an identity marker and as an expression of postcolonial reform. But Izala leaders asserted that their vision had been indispensable and they threw their support behind Ahmad Sani, the first governor to implement sharia. It's telling, too, that several Sufi scholars in Kano opposed the sharia project altogether, and at least one Sufi on the Kano State's sharia implementation committee resigned because of its Salafi domination.

Kano also created a Hisbah religious police to enforce sharia in parallel with the regular, state-run police, and its first leader was Aminudeen Abubakar, an Islamic University of Medina alumnus, student of Dr. Gumi, and prominent Salafi imam at the Dawah Juma'at Mosque in Kano.

Today, the twelve states administered by sharia have a mixed record. In Kano, the Hisbah imposes dress codes, busts bars and brothels, and adjudicates marital disputes. Under the aegis of sharia, people have been jailed for blasphemy, homosexuality, and suspicions of atheism. At the same time, popular support for sharia remains high in a region where the secular state still has a serious deficit of authority. Sharia is not going anywhere— and that's due in part to the vision and action of Izala.

From Medina to Maiduguri

In April 2014, Boko Haram kidnapped 276 female students from their school in Chibok, in the northeastern state of Borno. The event horrified and stunned observers within and without Nigeria, who had to shake their heads at the inability of the state to both protect the girls and negotiate with the terrorist group for their inscrutable demands. Boko Haram has kidnapped over 1,000 children in further incidents since 2018 and, as recently as 2018, abducted 110 more girls from the town of Dapchi. Even during one of my visits in May 2019, a handful of staffers were kidnapped from a girls' school in Zamfara State.

Easily the most infamous Islamic movement in northern Nigeria, Boko Haram has been responsible for, in addition to countless terror attacks and kidnappings, a devastating regional famine. Since Boko Haram styles itself as a Salafi-jihadist group, it begs the question of how closely it is linked with the greater Salafi movement in the region, and of whether that Salafi movement would have flourished in northern Nigeria without Saudi dawa.

In a word, the answer is no. Saudi proselytizing has been integral to Salafism in northern Nigeria, and Boko Haram's ideology directly springs from the Salafi corpus spread by Saudi-educated Nigerian preachers. Its founder even took refuge in Saudi Arabia. But in an ironic twist, the majority of mainstream Nigerian Salafis oppose the jihadi group and have even tried to wage public debates with its leaders, albeit to little effect. The

102   resulting situation is typical of Saudi proselytization in the wild, which often ends up with unstable by-products.

Boko Haram's Violent Turn

Although Boko Haram has praised Al Qaeda and pledged allegiance to ISIS in 2015, it remains more a localized insurgency than a transnational jihadist group. In fact, it existed for six years as a nonviolent fundamentalist group and only turned violent in 2009, when its founder was killed. Its context is deeply local to Maiduguri, the northeastern state where it is headquartered. And Salafism would never have entered Maiduguri were it not for a preacher named Jafar Adam.

Jafar Adam was the most popular and charismatic Saudi-educated Salafi in modern Nigeria. Although he was from a humble background, he went to Medina with a scholarship to IUM in 1988, around age twenty-seven, after winning a Quran recitation competition in Kano. He was hand-picked for this by a Saudi official named Muhammad Abd Allah Zarban al-Ghamidi, who was on one of the regular Saudi recruiting trips to Nigeria. Adam returned to Nigeria as a fiery preacher, determined to propagate Wahhabi doctrine. He joined Izala and preached at a mosque in Kano financed by the British-Saudi NGO called Al-Muntada al-Islami. He quickly attracted an avid following for his charismatic sermons and debates with Shia and Sufi leaders. He preached from the core Wahhabi texts of Ibn Abd al-Wahhab and al-Albani but enthralled listeners by explaining them in colloquial Hausa. He was a key figure in Kano's sharia implementation committee in 2000.

Eventually, he was recruited to preach at a new mosque in Maiduguri built by a Nigerian oil multimillionaire named

Mohammad Indimi. Adam traveled there every few months to give his signature *tafsir,* or explications, of the Quran. Salafism would likely not have reached Maiduguri, the capital of Borno State, without Adam's preaching. In the 1970s, there was an attempt to transfer the fiery Izala founder Ismail Idris to Borno, but it failed due to grassroots resistance there. The charismatic Adam managed to forge essentially a "new frontier" for Salafism in Maiduguri in the 1990s, according to the scholar Andrea Brigaglia, who has reconstructed Adam's biography.

"The trouble started when Adam was installed as a preacher at the new mosque in town," recalled Aliko Ahmed, a businessman from Maiduguri who now lives in Kano. "He created his own group, separate from Izala, called Ahl Al-Sunna, and it became hugely popular, even among my friends." Ahl Al-Sunna considered itself more purely Salafi, and less tainted with politics, than Izala had become by the new millennium.

Adam's star student was a young man named Muhammad Yusuf. Adam considered Yusuf as his protégé and appointed him to lead Ahl Al-Sunna's youth wing in Maiduguri. But just as Adam branched off from Izala in a more hardline direction, Yusuf did exactly the same to Adam. Rejecting Adam as also insufficiently Islamic, he established the Ibn Taymiyya Center in Maiduguri, named after the medieval theologian who is revered by Salafi and Wahhabis. In 2007, he published the foundational manifesto of Boko Haram: "This is our creed and method of proclamation," which mostly consisted of quotations from Saudi Salafi texts. Boko Haram was not his own name for the group. He called it *Jama'at Ahl as-Sunnah lid-Dawah wa'l Jihad,* the Group of the People of the Sunnah for Preaching and Jihad. Nigerian media came up with the shorter cognomen, which captured Yusuf's central idea that Western education, or "Boko" in Hausa, was forbidden.

This newer, even more charismatic breakaway movement drew hundreds more young people. Everyone in Maiduguri knew Yusuf, said Ahmed, and vice versa. "Once I met him in a gas station and he instantly recognized me and asked whether I was still part of the army of Satan," meaning, whether he was still resisting Yusuf's Salafi movement.

Yusuf was investigated by the government for his extreme rhetoric in 2004 and briefly fled to Saudi Arabia, like many a fiery preacher who seeks refuge. (Recall that Indonesia's Habib Rizieq remains in Saudi Arabia too.) Before and after that, he continued to pick up thousands of followers across the northeastern states and even from neighboring countries like Niger, Chad, and Cameroon.

But within a few years, this volatile Salafi coterie in Maiduguri became an ouroboros, the snake that eats its own tail. In 2007, Jafar Adam, the most influential Saudi-educated nonviolent Salafi preacher of the new millennium, was assassinated under mysterious circumstances—most likely on the directive of Boko Haram, the extremist group formed by his student. And then, in 2009, Boko Haram clashed with the Nigerian military due to suspicion that it was developing bombs. One thousand people died, seven hundred in Maiduguri alone. Among them was Muhammad Yusuf, who was interrogated by police and then executed. That was when the group took its deadly turn.

The heavy-handed military confrontation was the proximate cause for this turn. But in the bigger picture, it's obvious that Boko Haram could not have formed as a group, nor attracted its base of thousands across multiple states, without its ideological background and the charismatic preachers at its core.

Boko Haram's material links to Saudi and Gulf actors are basically opportunistic. Around 2002, Osama bin Laden reportedly sent an aide to Nigeria with $3 million to distribute among local groups including Boko Haram. In 2015, Boko Haram switched allegiance to the Islamic State and restyled itself as the "Islamic State in West Africa."

It's worth noting that, in its current, violent iteration, Boko Haram considers Saudi Arabia to be a state of unbelief. Under the leadership of Abubakar Shekau, who took over from Yusuf in 2009, Boko Haram declared its enmity with literally every other Islamic group and entity imaginable, including the Sufis, Shia, Izala, the Nigerian government, and the Kingdom of Saudi Arabia. In a video message filmed in December 2014, Shekau, holding a rifle that he periodically shot off to punctuate his address for emphasis, screamed, "The Saudi state is a state of unbelief, because it is a state that belongs to the Saud family, and they do not follow the Prophet . . . the Saudi Arabians, since you have altered Allah's religion, you will enter hellfire!"

Saudi Arabia was the site of an attempted negotiation between Boko Haram and the Nigerian state in 2012 to 2013. Perhaps unsurprisingly, the peace talks held there did not make much headway.

The Yan Medina
Jafar Adam was part of the Yan Medina, the "Medina people," so-called since so many prominent clerics studied at IUM (although the term refers more broadly to the Nigerian graduates

106 of Saudi universities). Beyond supporting Gumi and the subsequent rise of Izala, Saudi Arabia's other dawa priority in Nigeria was to distribute scholarships. By the 1990s, there were at least one hundred Saudi alumni in northern Nigeria and they have had an outsize influence on both its religion and politics, often blurring the line between the two. A case in point was Jafar Adam serving on Kano's sharia implementation board.

Since the Boko Haram insurgency started, Saudi officials stopped coming on personal recruiting trips, said Dr. Abdullah Pakistan, the regional head of Izala and an IUM graduate, whom I met at his home in Kano. He is a perfect example of a Saudi alumnus abroad who joins a Saudi-supported organization (Izala) and maintains rich ties to the kingdom. He wore a loose two-piece *babagida* suit favored by Hausa men made of light-blue satin and sat on a long, brown pleather couch in the semi-darkness of a power outage. His mosque in Kano is named after Jafar Adam, whose death was felt deeply in the Salafi community. "Adam went his own way," noted Dr. Pakistan, referring to his breakaway from Izala, but they maintained good relations.

Pakistan studied Quranic exegesis in Medina from 1981 to 1985 and was the first Nigerian to study the subject there. He was recruited through a dawra tour and took four entrance exams. "But they were actively looking for people to study, so even if you didn't have complete credentials, you could still go," he said. He had already learned some Arabic at school in Kano, so he was handily qualified.

"Oh, I loved it in Medina," he said. "They give you all the textbooks, and even a ticket to visit home for two months every year . . . and there were no strikes or disturbances." In those years, Nigeria was rocked by military coups, so this was no small attraction. IUM students could also take a pilgrimage to Mecca as often as once a week, if they wanted to. "It makes you so happy," he said, with obvious pleasure.

Nigerians who come home from Saudi Arabia can only really work in the fields of teaching, preaching, or Arabic-language instruction, said Pakistan. He went for further study in Islamabad, where he acquired his unusual alias, to distinguish himself from the scores of other people named Abdullah in Kano.

When he himself finally came home, he joined and quickly rose up through the Izala ranks to become the leader of its Kano branch. He also became a Saudi university recruiter himself, spending thirty to forty days each year scouting promising students from states like Sokoto and Kano. He also gave Islamic pedagogy lessons to local primary and secondary school teachers.

Today, he said, Izala still has an active relationship with Saudi Arabia. There is a large Saudi consulate in Kano, to which he suggests good locations to build mosques, usually in places far outside the metropolitan center, like Gwarzo, in the far west. (A Gwarzo resident later confirmed that the mosque in Lakwaya village was expanded and renovated by Saudi aid in 2002.) "Not less than one per month," he said, of his recommendations for new mosques, over the last five years. Then he helps staff those mosques with Izala-affiliated imams. "There are so many people waiting on standby," he said, "so it's easy." Izala doesn't maintain a registry, but its membership was estimated to be about two million in the 1990s and remains several million people strong today.

Other members of the Yan Medina, which is to say mainstream Salafis, tried to debate Boko Haram in its early years.

108   Dr. Isa Ali Pantami, a Salafi who taught computer science in
      Medina, challenged Muhammad Yusuf to a public debate in
      2008. Although they both considered themselves Salafis at
      the time, Pantami was unnerved that Yusuf also believed, for
      instance, that democracy was incompatible with Islam, that the
      earth orbited the sun, and that vaccines were un-Islamic. They
      debated for six hours; Pantami was thirty-six and Yusuf was
      thirty-one. "I won the debate," Pantami told me in Abuja, where
      he now directs the National Information Technology Develop-
      ment Agency. "But Yusuf died a year later, and in the long run,
      it didn't stop Boko Haram from evolving into the terror group
      that it became."

      The issue was that, in the early 2000s, much of Yusuf's
      preaching related to jihad was identical to that of nonviolent
      mainstream Salafis like Jafar Adam and Kano's Salafi preachers.
      They all, for instance, basically supported suicide bombing. The
      scholar Abdulbassit Kassim notes that the "enemy-centric the-
      ology" central to Yusuf's preaching was institutionalized by
      the Salafi clerical establishment based in Kano. So, when the
      thriving Salafi establishment tried to draw a line in the sand
      about acceptable and unacceptable extremisms—much like
      Saudi Arabia itself has tried to do countless times—they failed
      to meaningfully counter it.

      Boko Haram has traumatized northern Nigeria and, under
      its new iteration as the Islamic State of West Africa, is nowhere
      near eradicated. Its geographic base has shrunk, but it has killed
      over 35,000 people and displaced millions more. The group is
      said to have imposed a "level of destruction unseen since the
      country's civil war in the late 1960s."

As recently as three years ago, even central Kano was a ghost town, stopped up by checkpoints throughout the city, recalled Dr. Lawi Atiku, a prominent Sufi scholar. Atiku's son was gunned down by Boko Haram insurgents in 2014, at age eighteen, while praying in a Kano mosque.

"They take our children physically and then steal the minds of even more youth," said Aliko Ahmed. He had to flee Maiduguri in 2009 because of his now-defunct blog, which was critical of the militancy and subjected him to severe death threats. His voice broke. "Our society is full of holes now."

A Big Wedding

On May 4, 2019, on somewhat short notice, I was invited to a wedding. It would be held the next day, at the Emir's Mosque in Kano, followed by a reception at the governor's residence. There would be five hundred brides and five hundred grooms.

It was a Kano State mass wedding, a popular government program started in 2013 to marry off widows and divorcées. The new couples get medical exams, cash, and new furniture to start their new life. In return, they have to promise never to get divorced. Many factors aligned behind this seemingly odd program. Kano, like many northern states, has an extremely high divorce rate; a third of marriages are estimated to fail within six months. There is widespread polygamy in the Sahel region, where men can marry up to four wives, which some say contributes to the culture of impermanence around marriage. With the advent of sharia, there was a renewed desire to curb "vice" and especially extramarital sex. So the Kano government, together with the state's Hisbah (the religious police), have come up with the perfect solution: subsidizing marriages en masse. The program perfectly unites the "progressive desire to care for the vulnerable and the Salafi desire to prevent extramarital sex," per one scholar of Nigerian Salafism, Alex Thurston.

Mass weddings exemplify the ordinariness and practicality of sharia in Kano. The Hisbah was led until 2019 by a prominent Salafi, Aminu Daurawa, who didn't study in Saudi Arabia but came up the Salafi intellectual climate led by the Yan Medina. By the 2010s, Salafis were firmly ensconced in the government and, furthermore, Salafi social ideals were being put into practice everywhere.

I stood in the sandy courtyard of the Emir's mosque on Sunday as the grooms, all dressed in blinding white silk *babar rigas*, filed in for their wedding benediction. The mosque was low to the ground and had a squat teal dome. Women were not allowed inside, but I watched the entrance of imperious Emir of Kano, a billionaire businessman wearing a truly extravagant rendition of the traditional Sahel turban, which wrapped around his chin and into a bulbous crown, topped with a springy bow.

The new Kano governor, Abdullahi Ganduje, addressed the grooms over the loudspeaker. It was expected to be a perfunctory benediction. He said, "We are going to reorganize the Hisbah Command as it has deviated from its established norms." The listeners in the courtyard stirred. "Corruption, mismanagement, treachery, and other ills have eaten deep into the fabric of the Command's leadership," the governor continued. "We will not allow this to continue under our watch."

I slowly realized I was not at a Hisbah event at all. The governor and the state government had just usurped the occasion to marginalize the religious police of Kano. This mass wedding, for the first time ever in Kano, was a project of only the state government, with no input from the religious police. It was a symbolic wresting of social functions away from the Hisbah and back to the central government. I had come hoping to see the Hisbah's Salafi ideals in practice, but had witnessed something else entirely.

We continued on to the governor's palace, where I sat on plastic chairs on the women's side of the plaza, next to Binta, a twenty-three-year-old divorcée in a black spangled hijab, who met her thirty-five-year-old husband five months ago and hoped to marry him quickly and start a new life. She hadn't told any of her friends about the relationship yet. She had almost no money for a second wedding and was grateful that this was free. Another bride, a beautiful thirty-year-old Yoruba woman named Rashidat, was reconciling with her first husband, with whom she had two children. One of her kids, a boy named Mubarak, was on her lap. She had thin, Garboesque eyebrows. When they reconciled, they applied to the government to be considered for the mass ceremony. Her groom is a Hausa man from Kano and they speak to each other in English. "It will be nice to get the family back together," she said. Behind them were hundreds of plastic-wrapped mattresses, cupboards, and velour arm chairs, baking in the sun.

I scanned the program and saw that the name of Aminu Daurawa, the ultra-popular Salafi preacher, had disappeared. It turned out that he had recently been fired from the Hisbah. An official who worked in the governor's office later told me he suspected that Daurawa had been sidelined because he was too personally charismatic and too close to the previous governor.

     At first, I was disappointed not to see the Hisbah in action, but I realized that the evolution of the mass wedding perfectly shows how a Salafi project was mainstreamed by the government in Kano. Salafi ideas and ideals were crucial during the sharia implementation period of the new millennium, but now the government has cut out the middle man and upholds these ideals on its own.

I noticed, too, that while the Hisbah had been cut out from the occasion, Dr. Pakistan was still invited, on behalf of Izala. So that group seemed to be still in the government's good graces. It's complicated to keep track of the shifting power balances between religious and governmental groups in northern Nigeria, but it's important to do so to fully understand the malleable effects of Saudi dawa here and its constantly evolving Salafi movement.

Today, said Dr. Pakistan, Izala is more accepting than in its early years—even of Sufis—and he offered, vaguely, that, "If you believe in the Quran, you're in Izala." Izala briefly split into two factions in the 1990s, after Dr. Gumi's death, and since its reconciliation in 2011, has been careful to present a united front. Today, said Pakistan, Izala focuses on only one activity: "Teaching people."

Besides, Izala has no need to be as combative now as it was in the 1980s because it broadly won the war of ideas. Its vision of northern Nigeria's future is the present. Izala has hundreds of mosques today and, unlike at the time of its founding, can influence official sharia. In forty years, it has created a bloc that competes with, and even sets the terms of the relation to, centuries-old Sufi brotherhoods. Izala's very name calls for the "Re-establishment of the Sunnah," the traditions of the Prophet, and in many ways, they got that.

Beyond the dawa activities of the Saudi consulate in Kano, which Dr. Pakistan explained, Saudi Arabia is also building a massive new complex for its Kano consulate on Ahmadu Bello Way, down the road from its present building. The complex, whose construction started in early 2015, is designated as the "consul's residence and staff housing" and includes several massive gray buildings with twenty-four-hour security. It's being built by a Turkish company, Kurortno Strotelstvo Limited, and was still not open as of late 2019, two years after its due date. The massive new consulate may be a sign that Saudi dawa will once again increase in Kano.

The main Saudi embassy in Abuja distributes Qurans printed in the King Fahd Complex in Medina, in Hausa, Yoruba, and even Ebira, a language spoken in central Nigeria. The Saudi Dawa Ministry supported 9,395 preaching sessions, 301 prison visits, 460 seminars, 1,321 tours, and 18,993 lectures in Nigeria in 2016–17, and Nigeria was second only to Sudan on the list of countries where the ministry works in Africa.

Although Sufis in northern Nigeria still associate Salafis with money, Saudi charity dried to a trickle here after 9/11, just as it did in Indonesia. As a case in point, the entire office of the Muslim World League in Nigeria, in Abuja, is just one person.

"It's just you?" I asked Dr. Fadul Khulod, at the MWL office in Abuja, in a bright, one-story building off Aminu Kano Crescent. Sixty-two-year-old Khulod is the first and last employee of MWL Nigeria. "We've had a lot of budget cuts," he said, apologetically, as I entered his spare office. He docs still have three

114   security guards, who alternate eight-hour shifts so the building has round-the-clock security. "But not even a cleaner, anymore."

Khulod was hand-picked by MWL officials in Mecca to set up this office in 1992. He had a square jaw dotted with gray stubble and wore bifocals. He grew up in Sokoto, got a PhD at Al-Azhar in Cairo, and taught at the Islamic University in Niger that was founded by the Saudi-affiliated Organization of Islamic Countries in 1974. While on pilgrimage in Mecca, he met Dr. Umar Masif, then the president of MWL, who said they were looking for a native Nigerian to set up a real office in Abuja. (At that point, MWL funds were still being informally dispensed by Dr. Gumi.) MWL Nigeria runs several schools today in northern cities including Figbo, Ibadan, and Inuri.

"A lot of the [Nigerian] Saudi university graduates came to teach in our schools, but it was under the Saudi embassy's watch, which had a huge headache dealing with their salaries and so on. That's why they brought me in," said Khulod. He took charge of the budget allocated to Nigeria from Mecca and distributed it among the schools. One of his first actions as its president was to go on a road trip to every school that claimed to be on the MWL payroll and confirm that they really existed. (There were at least five phantom schools.) The largest MWL-funded school today, Madrasatu al- Dawatu al -Islamiyah in Ibadan, has 3,500 students.

Khulod speaks crisp, British-adjacent English and his office was full of boxes of Al-Hasa dates from Saudi Arabia's Eastern Province. It is a signature Saudi charity move to send boxes of dates to its beneficiaries worldwide, which harkens back to the era before the 1973 oil embargo, when dates were still the kingdom's third-biggest export, after oil and crude.

"I do it because I have to," said Khulod, of his job. He can't afford a secretary and still personally translates MWL headquarters' missives, from Arabic into English, for circulation in Nigeria. After 9/11, all Saudi charities in Nigeria were subject to extensive review, or, as Khulod understood it, "Bush said he had to check every Islamic school." That took a decade. He said MWL Nigeria's schools received no money at all for fifteen months between 2002 and 2003. That was when he let go of most of his staff and worked with a skeleton crew. During the decade of scrutiny, he said, dozens of the Muslim World League's global offices were closed, so he counted himself lucky. Did he resent the investigation? "No," he said simply. "Rabita is a very clean organization," he said, using the shorthand for the League's Arabic name, Rabitat al-Alam al-Islami. "We can handle any inspection."

Most of what MWL does in Nigeria today is centered on education: running schools, putting on evening classes for adults, staging occasional missionary and conversion activities in those schools, and distributing English-language Qurans from Saudi Arabia that are sent from MWL headquarters. "Converting people is part of our assignment," said Khulod. Sometimes he works with the International Islamic Relief Organization, which was founded by MWL but is now discrete. One of the MWL schools in Figbo switched affiliation to IIRO in 2009. Their schools have been teaching the general national curriculum since 1982, but MWL still sends them library books.

Khulod also used to run a month-long teacher training conference for Islamic teachers from all over West Africa, who were instructed by visiting Saudis, and where everyone in attendance got a $500 stipend. That ended around 2012, after the dry times

116   took their toll. These days, he instead recommends teachers and promising Arabic students to attend short educational courses of up to nine months in Mecca.

I asked Khulod if he has any plans to retire. "As long as someone is breathing, he should not retire," he said. "After all, the Prophet was also useful until the end of his life."

Khulod grew up in a nomadic Shuwa Arab family in northeastern Nigeria and recalls learning Arabic while sitting on a dirt floor. He still keeps a handwritten Quran from his hometown in his office. In contrast, he said, the MWL school graduates are "amazing." They have learned from both an Islamic and national curriculum, come out speaking and writing both English and Arabic, and can "go on to higher study anywhere in the world."

We met about a week before Ramadan and he was fretting about how to service the poor families that MWL typically helps during the fasting month. "We used to be able to help four or five hundred families every single day of Ramadan, giving them rice, sugar, Indomie [instant noodles]," he said, but he has since downsized to small cash handouts to families in severest need. "Without money," he said, "we can only do so much." He has not scouted a successor.

The Thousand-Day Protest

"We will never surrender! Allah is our defender!" the protesters sang, in English. They were in Abuja during Ramadan, when the traffic congeals over the course of the afternoon; the shadows elongate as cars pile up, everyone leaving work early because no one wants to be caught on the road when they can finally break the fast. Under the overpass, a crowd of hundreds of young Nigerians marched down the main road in neat lines. At the very front, three young men held a banner that said "BUHARI: FREE ZAKZAKY/ TO ATTEND TO HIS HEALTH CONDITION."

The person the protesters wanted Nigerian President Muhammadu Buhari to free was the country's most prominent and most controversial Shia cleric: Ibrahim Yaqoub El Zakzaky, who leads the Islamic Movement in Nigeria, or IMN. Now designated by the Nigerian government as a terrorist group, IMN started as a campus movement in the 1970s at Ahmadu Bello University in Zaria that advocated for military-ruled Nigeria to become an Islamic caliphate. After Zakzaky visited Iran in the 1980s and converted to Shiism in a fit of revolutionary

118   fervor, his movement became distinctively Shia. It is now a two-million-strong group with a highly organized regional structure. And it has long been marked by a propensity toward violent confrontation: by 1999, fewer than two decades after its founding, at least seventy-nine members had been "martyred" by police and the military. IMN members honor these fallen with specially composed Hausa poems and in a book of martyrs, *Mu'assasatus Shuhada*. There is even a charitable arm of IMN called the Shuhada Foundation to support the children and relatives of dead members.

The worst clash to date came in 2014, when the Nigerian military killed at least 348 IMN followers, including three of Zakzaky's sons, in the three-day Zaria massacre.

I met thirty-two-year-old Abdullahi Muhammad Musa, who watched five of his family members die in Zaria, in Abuja's modern business district of Wuse. Slim, with dark skin, a puff of black hair, and smiling eyes, Abdullahi now helps organize the daily protests. He wore two silver rings set with gemstones, which is known here as a distinctive Shia affectation. He recounted going up to Zaria on the second day with his family. Meaning, once the killings were already underway, I asked him. "Yes, after they started. When we heard about the attack, it convinced us to go there more, because people were trying to kill our leader," he explained. Musa joined IMN when he was in grade school in Abuja, along with his mother, who attended Zakzaky's sermons in the capital and became a devoted follower.

"I drove up to Zaria with my three nieces, Ayesha, Fatima, and Nusaiba, plus Ayesha's husband, Buhari, and their two-year-old daughter," he said. They arrived on Saturday night to a chaotic scene. IMN's headquarters, known as the Hussainiyya, had already been raided. They went on to the Fudiyya Islamic Center to regroup with other members, from where they heard explosives and moved preemptively toward Zakzaky's house. They passed the night there until 4 a.m. A few hours later, on Sunday morning, the military started to advance again.

"The army surrounded the house and began shooting on arrival. There was no conversation. Their target was the Shaykh," said Musa, using the honorific most IMN members use for Zakzaky. "They had orders to bring him back to Abuja dead or alive." Thinking that the army wouldn't attack unarmed citizens, many IMN members, including Abdullahi and his family, physically guarded the Shaykh. "But we were wrong," he said. "They were even using grenades." Abdullahi's niece Fatima stepped forward from a human chain and a soldier shot her down on the spot. The rest of his family members went down in short order. Abdullahi was narrowly spared because he was wearing the ID card of the National Youth Service Corps, a Teach for America–like program through which he was teaching high school chemistry in Kwara State. But soldiers killed almost everybody else in the house and set the residence ablaze for good measure. "There's even a safehouse nearby where we were treating injured people, and they set that on fire, too," said Abdullahi.

Abdullahi was released a couple of days later and he hitch-hiked back in a daze to his school in Kwara. He called his mother to tell her what had happened, and she had a stroke within hours, which left her half-paralyzed until her death in 2019.

The Zaria massacre exploded the legend of Zakzaky, already a hugely charismatic figure. "You know," one of his followers told me gleefully, when I struck up a conversation in a hotel

120 restaurant after seeing an IMN pin on his bag, "one of his eyes was gouged out by the military. And he just"—he stuck a finger in the orbit of his eye—"popped it back in!"

"How do you kill someone and they don't die? That's the question," said Abdulmumin Gawi, in a typical rendition of the Zakzaky legend. Gawi is a journalist with IMN's Hausa-language newspaper, *Al-Mizan*, who lives in Kano. Gawi was planning coverage of the Zaria massacre with a friend, Ibrahim Usman, on the first night of the killings. Usman went from Kano to Zakzaky's house on Sunday morning, thinking the worst was over, but was promptly gunned down, alongside Abdullahi's family. Like many IMN members, Gawi is convinced that the government basically laid a trap for Zakzaky in Zaria. He notes that there were several other Quds Day protests in Nigeria but military only showed up to the one procession. "And what even took them to the Shaykh's house, which is several kilometers away from the procession?" asked Gawi. "Clearly, the whole thing was designed to take out the Shaykh. They thought they could finish it on that day," he mused, "but it took them many days, and they didn't even succeed."

Zakzaky gave an interview to BBC Hausa while he was under siege on that Saturday night saying that "only God could save him." He was taken into police custody in Abuja, and ever since January 2016, his followers have protested in the capital city, every single weekday, for almost four years, cycling through various neighborhoods in hopes of attracting attention from the lawmakers whom they say have unjustly imprisoned their leader. The Constitutional Court ordered his release in early 2016, but the military ignored it and Zakzaky remains in jail. The Abuja protests precipitated more violence: fifty-four more protesters were killed in clashes with the police in the last four years. The Zakzaky affair has raised solidarity protests across the Shia world, from places like Lucknow and Chennai in India, as well as rolling coverage from Iranian news outlets.

Last May, the IMN protest in Abuja was shorter than usual because fasting in the damp heat kept energy levels low. The protesters made a long loop around the freeway divider and wrapped it up within an hour. Their protests are often criticized as disruptive and IMN is uniquely combative among Nigerian Shia movements. But it's also unique that hundreds from their movement have been killed with impunity and that their leader is imprisoned by the state. The nearly 350 people killed in the Zaria massacre were unceremoniously dumped in a mass grave. Some of them, claimed Gawi, were buried alive.

The sustained attack on this Nigerian Shia movement is one stark arena for the ideological proxy war between Iran and Saudi Arabia, Shia and Sunnah. While the Nigeria military ultimately carried out the massacre, the sentiment of the anti-Shia crusade in Nigeria was raised almost single-handedly by its new generation of Salafis nursed by Saudi dawa. "The stigma against IMN was rolled into sectarianism between Sunni and Shia," said Gawi.

At sunset, when the protest dispersed, I piled into a car with Abdullahi and his friends as they went to break their fast at the house of Fateema Yusuf, a soft-spoken woman and IMN member who wore a lilac *chador*. Her house was in a quiet compound and it was dark from yet another power outage. Her nine-year-old son, Muhammad, was bouncing off the walls, and I asked him if he ever went along to the protests with his parents. "Oh yes," he said, in between cartwheels in and out of the wide-open front door. "It's fun. We sing and dance."

122   Fateema brought out sliced fruit and fried yams for Abdullahi and his friends, Muhammad and Nurhudin. Muhammad had actually grown up in the Iranian holy city of Qom, where his father studied for a PhD, and was a second-generation Nigerian Shiite.

I asked them how they felt about spending years of their twenties protesting day in and day out. Muhammad said: "It's normal now."

Just like in Indonesia, the Iranian Revolution left a deep impression in Nigeria. "The Shia answer questions," said Saleh Zaria, who leads the Rasulallah A'azam Foundation (RAAF), another popular Shia movement headquartered in Kano that, unlike IMN, has not faced too much of a violent backlash yet. Iran followed up the revolution with dawa in Nigeria and West Africa. Zaria studied in Qom from 1998–2002, on a scholarship, and before that, at an Iran-funded institute in Ghana. ("Not just for free—we also got a hundred-naira monthly stipend," he said.) There are also Hausa-language TV and radio stations broadcast from Qom, both fully staffed with Nigerians.

The revolution again prompted Saudi Arabia to ramp up its own Nigerian dawa and amplify its anti-Shia rhetoric. For instance, it funneled money to the Salafi-oriented Muslim Students Society. Many of the major Izala ideologues, who made their names by railing against Sufism, picked up the anti-Shia crusade in the 1980s. The popular Salafi cleric Jafar Adam debated the Shia cleric Malam Awal Taludi in 2003 in a debate that is still sold in markets today. And as recently as 2015, the Saudi-based TV channel Al Wesal produced a documentary warning against the spread of Shiism in Africa, particularly in Nigeria.

Exact numbers of Nigerian Shia are hard to come by and estimates range up to nine million, out of a national population of

about 191 million. Zaria said he was "comfortable defending" the
estimate of six million Nigerian Shia. But by any measure, they are
a minority. All Shia in Nigeria face some resistance, even if they
are not persecuted to the extent of IMN. "The Salafis simply hate
us," said Zaria. "Were it not for the Sufis, we would be eliminated."

What's unique about the anti-IMN crusade was that it
was mainstreamed by the Nigerian government. Some think
this betrays the Salafi sympathies of the Buhari presidential administration, which is led by a Muslim Northerner who
has appointed many prominent Salafis to his cabinet, and buttressed by the general acceptability of Salafi ideas in public discourse. Another reason IMN is more of a target than other Shia
movements is that it identifies most strongly with the Islamic
Revolution in Iran and not merely with Shia texts.

Many IMN members think that Saudi Crown Prince
Muhammad bin Salman was talking about Zakzaky and the
Nigerian conflict when he mentioned in a long interview with
Time that Saudi Arabia still actively tries to counter other
Muslim countries' influence abroad. What he said was, "We
drove them [Iran, the UAE, Egypt, Kuwait, Bahrain, Yemen,
and 'a lot of countries around the world'] out of Africa heavily,
more than ninety-five percent." For Nigerian Shia, the fact that
the African theater was still on Saudi royals' radar was itself
damning and, in their view, he was taking credit for the most
violent Sunni-Shia conflict in Africa today.

IMN members are at once spirited and hopeless. "We won't
stop protesting," said Gawi. "But how many more of us have to
die before anyone cares?"

Beyond the intolerance of Shia, conflict with Sufis has
also been a major effect of Saudi proselytization and a reliable

124   standby of Nigerian religious conflict today. Izala was of course premised on eradicating Sufi "innovation," as was the original Wahhabism in Saudi Arabia. Northern Nigerian Sufis and Salafis still periodically come to blows. Consider the following tale of two mosques in the Sabuwar Gandu neighborhood of Kano.

The first Sabuwar Gandu mosque was intended as another pop-up Izala mosque, like the hundreds that Izala has built since 1978. In 2003, the state government allocated a plot of land for a mosque in Sabuwar Gandu, a new residential suburb south of Kano's Ring Road. Izala members funded most of the mosque's construction, but then the Emir of Kano decided to appoint a Sufi judge, Yusuf Ali, as its imam. This didn't go down well at all with the Salafis. In 2006, when the mosque opened for prayers, more than five hundred Salafi protesters, some armed with knives and machetes, attacked the congregation. They were mobilized through an Izala center on Kano's Beirut Road. In November, none other than Jafar Adam gave a famous and dramatic lecture about the mosque controversy entitled "The Struggle between Falsehood and Truth," arguing that there was an anti-Salafi conspiracy at the highest levels of Kano government. The Salafis sued the emir and governor to challenge the appointment. Perhaps to avoid embarrassment, the emirate caved and granted the mosque to them. The Salafis promptly appointed a Saudi alumnus, Sheikh Garangamawa, as imam. And they triumphantly named the mosque after Jafar Adam.

Not to be outdone, the Sufis launched a community appeal and a Sufi businessman named Isa Karabiyu donated another piece of land, worth about fifty million naira (about $137,000), directly opposite the mosque. Within nine months, the Tijaniyya Sufis built a mosque of their own and reinstalled

Yusuf Ali as the imam. The rose-pink Sufi mosque went up
across the street from the peach stucco Salafi one, with just a
narrow stream to separate them.

"This was the first conflict of this kind that I can remember,
to go to the extent of the governor and a special committee,"
said Yusuf Ali, when I met him at his home in Kano. Ali is
well known for performing exorcisms, a Sufi practice hated by
Salafis. Toward the end of our chat, he tapped at his watch and
told me to wrap it up because he had a *djinn*-possessed congregant waiting to meet him after sunset.

The trouble did not end once each camp had its mosque.
They kept holding their midday prayers at exactly the same
time, 1 p.m., and the clash of the sermons on their loudspeakers
disturbed everyone in the neighborhood.

"Garangamawa called us enemies of the Prophet and apos-
tates," said Ali. Their congregants hated each other. Each imam
was scared to walk on the other side of the stream. This went
on for an astonishing eight years, until a congregant finally
brokered a truce between the two imams and the Sufi mosque
agreed to hold its prayers one hour later.

The Salafis clocked this, too, as a triumph, since it was not
they who were forced to accommodate the other. And although
these battles are physically waged outside the walls of Kano,
their message has seeped inside. Today, recordings of Adam's
famous Sabuwar Gandu lecture are sold to young men in central Kano's vast Kurmi Market, inspiring a new generation of
ideologues.

"Today they are called Salafis, yesterday Izala, and before that
Wahhabis," said Shaykh Ahmad Zulfai Abubakar Nawali, an

erudite Tijaniyya Sufi scholar and poet, at his housing compound in Kano. "Whatever you call them, they don't like us," he said. "They are against most of our Sufi activities: *wazifa* [devotional singing], *maulid* [celebrating birthdays, especially of the Prophet Muhammad and other religious leaders], *dhikr* [remembrance] . . . they call us *kafir* [unbelievers] and *mushriq* [polytheists] . . . but according to *my* Islamic religion, you don't call your brothers kafir and mushriq."

Nigeria's Sufi culture is better seen than explained, said Nawali. So he invited me back a few days later to attend a maulid for the late Tijaniyya leader Ibrahim Niasse, who is feted throughout West Africa. The maulid celebration was joyful and Nawali's tafsir session gave way to a big party in the compound, where everyone convened over huge vats of jollof rice and hard dates. At the same time, the event pointed to the deeply ingrained hierarchy and elitism of Sufism in the region. Because of the importance that Sufis place on lineages (like that of Niasse) and on sheikhs (like Nawali) as mediators of texts, as opposed to Salafis, who encourage all followers to study the Quran and Hadith themselves, Sufism could not help but to lose followers when the democratic, revivalist Salafi movement encroached on their home turf. The Sufis, perhaps out of complacency, were also late to understand the importance of mass media. While Salafis enthusiastically released cassette tapes, videos, and MP3s; freely used Facebook and Twitter; and are ubiquitous on TV and the radio, Sufis relied more on interpersonal networks. The popular Salafi cleric Aminu Daurawa has two million Facebook followers and a daily radio show at 8 a.m. where he cheerily dispenses religious advice to scores of

acolytes who call in from across the north. Meanwhile, most of
the elder Sufi sheikhs, including Atiku and Nawali, expressed a
fundamental distaste for mass media.

A younger generation of more combative Sufis has emerged
in recent years, in response to Salafi provocations. The Qadi-
riyya Shaykh Abduljabbar Kabara gave a speech in 2013, dressed
in chain-mail armor, promising to fight and evict Salafis from
Kano. On Facebook, he refutes Salafis based on their own texts,
like that of the medieval theologian Ibn Taymiyya. He presents
himself as a guardian of Sufism against Salafi incursions.

Still, Atiku believes that Sufis lost the war of ideas and
that the Izala and Salafi vision for the future has won. Any sub-
stantive debates now take place on their terms. He lamented
the fragmentation of the Muslim community most of all. Blasphemy accusations against Sufis have been on the rise, which
he linked to the Salafi attitude of excommunicating "incor-
rect" Muslims. For instance, a Tijani Sufi preacher named Abdul
Inyass caused an uproar in 2015 when he stated in a controversial sermon that even the Prophet Muhammad would respect
the Tijani Shaykh Ibrahim Niasse if he came back to Earth.
He was attacked by Salafis on social media who called for his
death; thousands of protesters stormed the small courthouse
where he was tried for blasphemy and burned it down. Inyass's
court-appointed lawyer, who was not particularly sympathetic
to his case, told me that what he had said was entirely within the
bounds of Sufi discourse, which is known for its high emotional
tenor and flights of hyperbole. In the end, the furor over his
case was so great that, even though he was sentenced to death
by hanging in the sharia court, he eventually had to be released

128   because it was impossible to give him a free and fair trial. "But," said Atiku, "such a thing would have never even gone to trial before the Salafis came to power."

Shaykh Jafar's Legacy

Saudi Arabia's material investments in Nigeria plummeted after 9/11 and the attendant scrutiny on Saudi foreign affairs. So why is the Salafi movement still so powerful? The answer, just as in Indonesia, is that the concentrated decades of Saudi cultivation had worked so well that Saudi-educated and -supported Nigerians were able to create their own, self-sustaining institutions, permeate the government, and gain a firm foothold in the religious sphere. When the external funding dried up, they had already discovered the traditional levers of power. Salafism is there to stay in Nigeria; the war of ideas has been won, even more forcefully than in Indonesia.

Recall that the Medina-educated scholar Jafar Adam, the most influential Salafi of his generation, was also one of the main voices on the Kano sharia implementation committee in 2000. His blurring of religious and political authority was a prelude to their pervasive admixture in contemporary northern Nigeria. When Adam was killed in April 2007 at age forty-seven, he was honored as a martyr in the Friday prayer of the Grand Mosque of Mecca, which was broadcast worldwide.

And Jafar's legacy is, if anything, even more powerful today than it was when he mesmerized Kano and Maiduguri residents in the early millennium. His followers have formed a Shaykh Jafar Islamic Documentation Center at Bayero University Kano, the region's preeminent university. They are all young men, in their thirties, erudite and professional. Most of them have PhDs, not just in Islamic Studies, but in engineering and computer science.

They started canonizing Adam well before he died. One Salafi physician named Ibrahim Datti used to trail Adam on the road transcribing his sermons, including the very last lecture of his life on a Thursday night in Bauchi. But Adam's assassination kicked the effort into high gear. Another Saudi-educated Salafi, Dr. Rijiyar Lemo, officially opened the Documentation Center at the Kano office of Al-Muntada Islamic trust, an NGO that has since been shut down for its alleged terrorist affiliations.

Working in teams of six to eight people, the documenters rigorously transcribed Adam's lectures, tracking their progress on a color-coded spreadsheet. They have already released the first few volumes, hardbacks with lime-green covers that are printed in Egypt and distributed to booksellers in Kano. Their initial print runs have almost sold out.

Kano's book markets, in fact, are a good place to see the explosion of grassroots interest in Salafism. Whereas Saudi Arabia was once the main agent flooding northern Nigeria with free Qurans and Salafi books railing against Shiism and the like, there is a thriving independent market for Salafi books now, and most, like the Jafar Adam lectures, are printed in Egypt, not Saudi Arabia. I walked through the open-air book market at Bayero University's august old campus with Sani Yakub Adam, a young researcher who has been studying the market for Islamic literature in Kano. Opposite the BUK mosque, on a flat dirt expanse, ten booksellers spread out their wares on cloths, some of them providing wood planks to sit on while we browsed. It

130   has never been so easy to consume Salafi ideas. In fact, the most popular way to consume Salafi "texts" now is to buy a blank USB and load it up with the MP3 files of sermons, according to Nasir Abb Al-Hassan, the youngest bookseller there. "What can I say," he told me. "It's the digital age."

Rebuilding
Kosovo

In October 2013, Lavdrim Muhaxeri appeared in a film called *Clanging of the Swords IV,* produced by ISIS. In it, the plump, red-bearded twenty-three-year-old from Kosovo destroys his passport and pledges allegiance to the nascent caliphate. The next year he posted photos beheading a man in Raqqa. From Syria, he posted dramatic *cris de coeur* on social media and privately messaged Balkan imams requesting impressionable young recruits. Over four hundred Kosovars answered his call and joined him in the next four years. There were so many ethnic Albanians in ISIS from Kosovo, as well as from Albania and Macedonia, that they got a dedicated Albanian-speaking unit.

Kosovo has a population of just 1.8 million. But the small nation, which was once part of Communist Yugoslavia and which declared independence from Serbia in 2008, has contributed more foreign fighters per capita to ISIS than any other country in Europe. Its recruitment rate was more than eight times as high as France, Europe's largest overall source of jihadists. This was despite the fact that Albanian Muslims, who constitute about 95 percent of the population of Kosovo, are not particularly known for religious fervor. How did jihadism take root in Kosovo?

In no small part it was due to the Saudi charities that helped rebuild postwar Kosovo and the Saudi-educated imams who created a considerable new Salafi ecosystem in a country whose religious sphere was being rebuilt almost from scratch. In 2014, the Kosovar government enacted a high-profile roundup of imams whom they accused of propagating extremist ideology and/or encouraged their followers to join the "jihad" in Syria. Several of them, like Enes Goga and Dr. Shefchet Krasniqi, were, unsurprisingly, Saudi alumni. These clerics found eager audiences in Kosovo's young—the youngest in Europe—underemployed, and disgruntled postwar population.

Saudi and other Gulf charities landed in Kosovo during and after the Yugoslav Wars in 1998 and 1999. The Kosovo War lasted for fifteen months between Yugoslavia, which was led by the Serbian president Slobodan Milosevic, and the Kosovo Liberation Army (KLA), which was supported by NATO. By the time the war ended in June 1999, through a controversial NATO bombing, over 13,500 Kosovars had died or gone missing and over 1.2 million had been displaced. Kosovo was Saudi Arabia's last major foreign relief effort before 9/11. Two years after the Saudi Joint Relief Committee set up shop in Pristina, the Twin Towers attack seriously damaged the global Saudi brand and the kingdom would never again be able to mount a multilateral relief and dawa campaign without global scrutiny.

Kosovo is not a large, regionally powerful Muslim nation like Indonesia or Nigeria. It only declared its independence from Serbia in 2008 and its statehood remains unrecognized by dozens of countries including India, China, Brazil, and Russia. But the case of Saudi Arabia in Kosovo shows how Saudi dawa can change a small nation as much as a large one. These investments were concentrated in a compressed period of twenty years, so one can grasp their whole shape. Saudi dawa helped Salafism find a place in Kosovo, but it also helped rebuild the religious life of a community whose piety was suppressed for nearly a century. The ISIS foreign fighters are just one end of a remarkable new base for Salafis in the Albanophone Balkans that arose in just about three decades. In other words, Saudi charities enabled a more general postwar Islamic revival in Kosovo that included, as it does in much of the world, some Salafis.

The rise of ISIS threw a wrench into Kosovo's domestic religious revival by rerouting a voluble minority into jihad. But even that is not a straightforward narrative, because quite a few Kosovars went to fight in the Syrian War before ISIS even existed, against the perceived injustices of Bashar Al-Assad. Assessing the Saudi legacy in Kosovo, and in the Balkans, requires constantly holding such nuance in mind.

Over the course of three trips to Kosovo, what I felt most acutely were not its considerable Yugoslav or Ottoman legacies, but a pervasive sense of unfinishedness. My phone confusedly tried to get onto the cellular networks of neighboring Albania and Slovenia and would not display the weather in Pristina; I couldn't place a credit card travel alert for the country, which uses euros despite not being in the European Union. There is no standard spelling of Pristina/Prishtina/Prishtinë or Kosovo/Kosova/Kosovë. And many of its small towns are plastered with USAID and UN signage, symbols of a prolonged and perhaps eternal reconstruction. The United Nations Interim

134   Administration Mission in Kosovo, indicated by its very name to be an interstitial body, still exists, while Kosovo is still not recognized as a UN member state.

The Relief Commission

In September 1999, four months after the Kosovo War ended, a Hungarian émigré and art historian named András Riedlmayer flew to Pristina to survey the archeological damage inflicted on religious monuments in Kosovo, which was part of the Ottoman Empire for 457 years and is dotted with beautiful low-domed mosques and Sufi dervish lodges. During the war, Serb forces categorically razed nearly half of them. (Most Kosovars can tell you exactly how many, offhand: 218 mosques and Islamic spaces, all catalogued in a popular book edited by Riedlmayer.) Serb forces also killed at least forty Muslim imams and religious leaders.

Before his trip, Riedlmayer stopped by the UNESCO office in The Hague to ask them how best to conduct an archeological survey that would be useful for relief efforts. They advised him to collect as many photos as possible of Kosovo's monuments right before the war so they could compare the damage. So when he got to his first stop in Kosovo, an old Ottoman town about an hour north of Pristina, he had several prewar photos of its mosques in his pocket.

He arrived in a rented Jeep and immediately noticed something strange: not only was the mosque damaged—though it had not been completely razed to the ground, a small victory—but it no longer had a cemetery. In all the old photos, the courtyard was full of Ottoman tombstones, which are typically slender stone planks like cricket bats, inscribed with calligraphy and capped with a turban-like stopper. Now there were none. Riedlmayer walked behind the main mosque and discovered a huge pile of gravestones, now crushed to rubble.

"We asked some of the kids who were playing in the court-yard and they said 'the Arabs' came with sledgehammers," said Riedlmayer. "They were told there would be no more humani-tarian aid until they smashed those tombstones, because it was 'un-Islamic.'" So they did exactly that.

Then Riedlmayer went on to Gjakova, near Albania, which was home to the ornate, sixteenth-century Hadum Mosque. Serb forces had already set fire to the wood portico, but the inte-rior, which was inlaid with elaborate floral murals, had been preserved. The Saudi reconstruction agency got a permit from the local reconstruction officials to restore the mosque and had started painting over the murals in austere white. Luckily, locals in Gjakova raised an outcry and the Saudis abruptly pulled out of the project. In the capital of Pristina, the Hasan Beg mosque was simply torn down and rebuilt in an anodyne modern style, with shops and a Saudi-run Islamic center on the ground floor. In Peja, Gulf charities smashed gravestones at the sixteenth-century Defterdar mosque.

Tombstones and decorations are the object of much Wah-habi ire; recall that the Wahhabis of the nineteenth century razed the historic tombs of the Prophet's family in Saudi Arabia to the ground. At one point, they even tried to destroy the black Kaaba shrine, in the direction of which the world's 1.2 billion Muslims pray every day.

Saudi charities' blunt approach to rebuilding Islamic structures in Kosovo seemed like salt in the wound after the protracted wartime attack on them. Their efforts were ampli-fied by the other Gulf charity players that had emerged in the

·

international scene like Kuwait and the UAE, although Saudi Arabia was still the wealthiest of them, with the biggest dedicated in-country staff, and thus led the pack. Their work went largely unchallenged because the relief efforts of Western countries and the UN were not very concerned with mosques and religious life.

"We really couldn't monitor the Gulf charities at the time," said Sabri Bajgora, an imam who leads the Islamic Community of Kosovo. "In the first couple of years, we were almost wholly administered by the UN Interim Administration Mission in Kosovo [UNMIK]. We took any kind of aid," he said. "It wasn't until 9/11 that we had a serious awareness of the ideology that some of the Gulf charities brought with their aid." And even despite that, the Islamic Community didn't seriously scrutinize foreign charities until about 2013.

Kosovo after the war was a surreal place. Cars did not have license plates and there was no standard currency. People used Serbian dinars, deutsche marks, US dollars, Swiss francs, and Albanian leks interchangeably. Riedlmayer, who now works in the Harvard Fine Arts Library, recalled, "Anyone who showed up in Pristina with a Jeep could call themselves an NGO."

The Saudi effort was decidedly more concerted than that. Saudi Arabia was one of the first countries to offer humanitarian aid to Kosovo in December 1998, flying in two planes with 120 tons of tents, dates, blankets, and prayer carpets, while fighting was still ongoing. By the summer of 1999, a Saudi C-130 Hercules relief aid plane was flying every single day from Jeddah or Riyadh to Tirana, the capital of neighboring Albania, to deliver supplies. (Most Kosovars today are ethnic Albanians and speak Albanian, so there is considerable exchange of people and ideas between the two countries. Even the Saudi embassy that services Kosovo today is in Tirana, although there is also a small diplomatic office in Pristina.)

Saudis also set up a large field hospital in Tirana that serviced victims from across Albania, Kosovo, and Macedonia. The Saudi-led Organization of Islamic Cooperation, with its fifty-three member countries in 1998, supported Kosovo's independence bid at the behest of Kosovo's grand mufti, Rexhep Boja, who lobbied the group at its global conference in 1998.

In 1999, King Fahd set up the Saudi Joint Relief Committee (SJRC) for Kosovo and Chechnya, personally chaired by the Interior Minister at the time, Prince Naif bin Abdul Aziz. It was the umbrella organization for charities including the Al-Haramain Islamic Foundation (AHIF), the International Islamic Relief Organization (IIRO), the Muslim World League (MWL), and the World Assembly of Muslim Youth (WAMY). By the time NATO troops were deployed in Kosovo in June, the SJRC had sent forty-one cargo planes of aid worth over $11 million. They solicited cash and material donations both inside and outside the kingdom. Saudi aid was a mixed bag of supplies and religious paraphernalia, including dates, milk, 42,000 blankets, 110,000 Albanian-language booklets on Islam, and cash donations worth about eight million euros, reportedly supporting 14,000 people within Kosovo and almost 18,000 refugees outside it.

After the war, the SJRC maintained a budget of about $1 million, which included funding 388 missionaries for reconstructing 37 mosques, and building two religious schools. Another school was set up for Kosovar refugees in Albania under the WAMY. Over the next decade, organizations based in

138   and financed by Saudi Arabia supported more than thirty specialized Quranic schools in Kosovo's rural areas. The kingdom also extended scholarships both for religious and non-religious studies, including for doctors. In the former Yugoslavia, only five students per year across all its constituent territories got to study at the Islamic University of Medina, and that was increased to about twenty per year, after the war, just from Kosovo.

     The scrutiny of Saudi charity is not a recent development; the SJRC engendered controversy almost immediately. The Committee was originally led by a Saudi named Wael Jalaidan, a former member of the Afghan mujahideen and a close associate of Osama bin Laden. Western charities and the Saudi committees regarded each other with mutual paranoia; the Saudi aid workers were accused several times of spying on the American office in 2000, and in April 2000, Italian troops raided the Saudi office in Pristina. Still, after a NATO raid in 2000, SJRC staff in Pristina simply laughed at suggestions of links to bin Laden. "We are a group of well-known charities supported by the Saudi Arabian government," said one person who worked there. "But people react strangely to Saudi Arabians."

The Bosnian Prequel

A key reason why Saudi Arabia was able to mobilize its relief infrastructure so quickly in Kosovo was because it came right at the heels of the Bosnian War, where the kingdom had mounted a massive relief effort worth at least $600 million. The kingdom's Bosnian relief commission was personally chaired by then-Prince, now-King, Salman bin Abdul Aziz. Bosnia was the first major Saudi destination after the Afghan jihad, and the full sweep of Saudi institutions like the Islamic Development

Bank and the Saudi Development Fund, plus charities like Al-Haramain and Benevolence International Foundation, all stepped in, funding kindergartens, schools, orphanages, Islamic centers, and mosques, supplying all of them with Salafi literature and/or teachers. The Saudi High Commission for Relief of Bosnia and Herzegovina also financed the translation of at least thirty different Salafi books from Arabic to Serbo-Croatian and distributed them for free.

The timing was perfect; just as the Afghan conflict was morphing into a civil war, the Bosnian conflict flared in the spring of 1992. American support for Saudi foreign policy was fading after the Cold War, so relief and charity became the official new face of Saudi internationalism.

Of course, the Saudi relief operation was never mere relief: most famously, some four thousand to six thousand mujahideen from countries including Saudi Arabia joined the Muslim Bosniaks as foreign fighters, hoping to re-create the thrills of the Afghanistan jihad. Abu Abdul Aziz, a Saudi veteran of the Afghan (and also Kashmir and Philippines) jihad led the Muslim forces, which included Nasir Ahmad Nasir Abdallah al-Bahri, Osama bin Laden's former personal bodyguard. After the war, several mujahideen stuck around and married Bosnian wives. Saudi Arabia also built a huge, $30 million mosque complex in Sarajevo called the King Fahd mosque—the largest mosque in the Balkans—and sent missionaries, books and Qurans, and so forth to postwar Bosnia. In 2001, a NATO raid into the Saudi High Commission office in Sarajevo turned up terrorist maps of Washington, D.C., with bull's-eyes and other damning material, so the charity had to tone down its operations.

140   It was in Bosnia that Saudi charities perfected the combination of *igatha* and dawa, relief and proselytization. Sometimes, the distribution of aid to women depended on their wearing the veil and for men on attending mosque or growing out their beards, according to the researcher Jonathan Benthall, who visited postwar Bosnia in 1998. Such practices were frowned upon by the ruling Bosnian Party of Democratic Action, which forcibly dismantled the foreign mujahideen unit in 1994.

Many staffers of Saudi charities in Bosnia migrated to Kosovo by the end of the decade. There was a fair amount of movement between Balkan charities at this time. The IIRO charity, in particular, helped Afghan veterans pivot to the Balkans. In 1992, Muhammad al-Zawahiri, brother of the Al Qaeda operative Ayman al Zawahiri, came to work in the Albanian branch of IIRO, and helped other former mujahideen get jobs with charities, orphanages, and clinics there. Al-Haramain also opened an office in Tirana, which would become notorious within a decade.

The Vilayet of Kosovo

A word that Albanians love, to the point where you can buy souvenir magnets of it in Pristina tourist shops, is "authochtonous." It means indigenous to a place, rather than imported through migration or colonialism. It's used in many contexts, including that ethnic Albanians were indigenous to their peninsula and not migrants, but today, many Kosovar Muslims use it to describe how their tradition of European Islam is so old as to be indigenous to their place.

Kosovo was the longest-held Ottoman territory in Europe and was part of the empire from 1455 to 1912. Albania followed shortly after, in 1479. Through their *vilayets*, provinces, Albanians became enmeshed with the Ottoman Empire and with the larger Muslim world. In a historical irony, one Albanian-Ottoman governor of Egypt, Muhammad Ali, crushed a Wahhabi uprising there in the 1840s. On the other hand, one of the key Wahhabi ideologues of the twentieth century was a man known simply as al-Albani, "The Albanian." Muhammad Nasir-ud-Dīn al-Albani was one of the first professors at the Islamic University of Medina, wrote several seminal books on quietist Salafism, and encouraged Wahhabis to identify as Salafis, advancing the Salafi-Wahhabi merger that is commonplace today. He later angered the stodgy Saudi clerical establishment and was forced to decamp for Syria, but his popular books are still found anywhere touched by Saudi dawa. One of his students, the Macedonian Bekir Halimi, is now one of the major Salafi imams in the Albanophone world.

Against the five-century backdrop of Islamic culture in Kosovo, it is striking how systematically Yugoslavia and Serbs eroded its religious life. Communist Yugoslavia (1945–1992), which had little patience for religion in general, tried to shoehorn Balkan Muslim identity into the Slavic Sunni traditions based in Sarajevo, marginalizing the Sufi heritage of Albanians in Kosovo. Even in the Yugoslav era, Saudi charities donated some funds for the region's Islamic centers, religious schools, and mosques, like an Islamic Centre in Zagreb, in modern-day Croatia. Things went from bad to worse once war broke out. Serbs used minarets as target practice and targeted Sufi leaders for murder.

Despite such brutal attacks, Western relief agencies, including the UN Mission, were not explicitly concerned with

142   this heritage, which left a fairly obvious vacuum for the Saudi relief committee. It is not surprising that Saudi aid was basically welcomed in Kosovo, even if with reservations.

Reconstruction

Pristina is an energetic, young city shaped by wide Communist-era avenues and outsized monuments. In the early 2000s, in a newly independent Kosovo, hardline imams like Dr. Shefchet Krasniqi would lecture behind the Yugoslav-era (and Yugoslav-named) Palace of Youth and Sports, a vast gray pyramidal complex with spikes running down the center like a spinal cord. Pristina became an unlikely theater for a religious revival when Saudi Arabian charities expanded their presence after the war. From 2001 to 2008, Kosovo was ruled by an interim government and in 2008, after its declaration of independence from Serbia, became a full democratic republic. Saudi investment continued through both phases. In 2009, Saudi Arabia recognized Kosovo's independence after the country's top cleric visited Prince Alwaleed bin Talal in Riyadh.

The SJRC set up headquarters in Pristina's Dardanija neighborhood, where, on any given night around 2005, "skills training" sessions for women were accompanied by lectures on the superiority of Arab culture and the need to emulate the behavior of the first Muslims. Al-Haramain was one of the Saudi charities that organized these knitting-circles-cum-Salafi-sermons for women in Pristina. One woman who attended these said the lessons involved convincing Kosovar Albanians that the revolutionary Albanian hero Skender Beg was a traitor to Islam and that all the key points of Albanian Islam originally came from Arabs. Thus, in those early years, Saudi dawa was often explicitly

Wahhabi, meaning that it advocated subservience to the House   143
of Saud and the traditions of the Najd region of Saudi Arabia.
Over the next decade, conservative Islam in Kosovo would lose
this specific Wahhabi cast in favor of a transnational Salafism.

Saudi charities also offered free classes in useful subjects
like English and computer science, filling a gap for young people
looking to rebuild their lives after years of war. In Gjilan, a small
town where twenty foreign fighters later went to Syria, Saudi
NGOs set up computer science courses that were followed by
mandatory religious lectures, said Iljaz Mustafa, the chief imam
of Gjilan. "Once the war started in Syria, I think that's why we
were not 'immune' to the ideology," he said. "It came to us in
such ordinary ways." Saudi charity was even more influential in
rural Kosovo, where the SJRC provided "food, jobs, and hope,"
whereas Western aid agencies did not.

Kosovo's deputy defense minister, Burim Ramadani, told
me that the era of peak missionary activity was between 2001
and 2007, before Kosovo declared its independence. Ramadani,
originally a journalist, started his career in government at the
Interior Ministry in 2007 and one of his first tasks was to conduct a national security survey drawing from the various local
police units in Kosovo. Something he highlighted in the report
was that, throughout Kosovo, policemen expressed anxiety
about Wahhabi proselytization and study groups.

"The reaction of MPs to this issue was awful," he said. "They
absolutely refused to hear this." Amidst all the other political issues that the interim government was navigating at the
time, his calls to address religious fundamentalism were hardly
a priority. He was also accused by imams of Islamophobia, even
though, like most Kosovars, he, too, identifies as Muslim.

As late as 2011, he said, it was impossible to talk about Salafism and Wahhabism in Kosovo. Nevertheless, he continued to keep tabs on the Saudi charities. "Quite a lot of money was sent to individual imams," he said. "And they systematically influenced the Islamic Community of Kosovo by making sure that graduates of Saudi universities were authorized to become imams at prominent mosques, like Ekrem Afdiu and Shefchet Krasniqi." It wasn't the absolute number of dollars spent that was important, he said, but the concrete and targeted dispersal of it. Saudi charities were good at identifying nodes of influence.

The SJRC distributed Salafi books through three branch offices in Pristina, Gjilan, and Prizren, starting right after the war ended in 1999. The books include Ibn Abd al-Wahhab's *Book of Tawhid* and the collected fatwas of the Saudi cleric Bin Baz. The Committee also built ninety-eight primary and secondary schools in rural Kosovo after the war. The most promising students were enrolled in thirty Quranic schools that were built in quick succession in the early 2000s by the Islamic Endowment Foundation, a Saudi charity under the SJRC umbrella. At least a hundred unlicensed mosques were built, by various entities, between 2002 and 2012, too. The construction of mosques remains poorly supervised to this day. The World Assembly of Muslim Youth facilitated dozens of scholarships for higher education in Saudi Arabia and many of the returning graduates immediately became imams in a country that faced a chronic shortage of them.

In early millennial Kosovo, there were both official Saudi charities and loosely affiliated groups with Saudi links. The Al-Haramain Islamic Foundation (AHIF), whose branches around

the world were raided after 9/11, spent nearly eighteen million euros in Kosovo between 1999 and 2005, according to its
records that were obtained by Kosovo's Zëri newspaper. It set up
shop in Pristina's Velania neighborhood in 1999 and went on to
repair twenty-eight schools (including six in Pristina, seven in
Gjilan, and nine in Prizren) at a cost of six million euros, build
200 homes and refurbish 269 more, and build nine mosques.
As part of the SJRC, Al-Haramain sent 360 tons of medicines
in 1999 through seven airplanes and fifteen barges. It repaired
ten health centers and funded twenty Kosovar doctors to study
medicine in Saudi Arabia. In November 1999, it funded the University Clinical Center of Kosovo to establish the "Prince of
Sultan's Laparoscopic Center," funded the training of its leader,
Dr. Faris el Hadi, and promised to cover its operating costs
for five years. But right after 9/11, the Pristina office of AHIF
destroyed most of its documents because the charity was under
scrutiny for its links to Al Qaeda, as former Secretary of State
Colin Powell noted in a 2003 memo to the CIA. Al-Haramain
also changed its operating name in Kosovo "at least ten times,"
after it was flagged as a terror financier by the UN, according to
one national police officer.

Al Waqf Al Islami, another big postwar charity, was headquartered in the Netherlands, but is led by a Saudi businessman
named Ahmad Al-Hussaini, who has been on its board of directors since 1991. As of 2014, its branch in Kosovo still received
regular requests from the president of the Islamic community of
Kosovo, Naim Ternava, to fund new mosques and help refurbish
old ones. These refurbishments were not ideologically neutral:
at one mosque in the village of Bajcine near Podujevo, Al Waqf

146 Al Islami wired $25,000 into the account of the Islamic Community of Kosovo, according to an investigation by Kosovar journalists Visar Duriqi and Artan Haraqija. The subsequent mosque renovation also entailed removing its anti-Wahhabi imam, Idriz Bilali. He was replaced by a Salafi imam named Fadil Sogojeva, known for stances like encouraging the segregation of unmarried men and exhorting women to cover their bodies up to their feet. The Kosovo branch of Al Waqf Al Islami was finally closed in August 2018, along with twenty other Islamic charities. The main headquarters of the charity has since been rebranded as the Al Abraar Foundation and is still based at Al-Furqaan mosque in the Dutch city of Eindhoven.

The only major non-Saudi Gulf charity working in Kosovo at this time was the Kuwait-based Revival of Islamic Heritage Society, which registered itself in Kosovo in September 2000, a few months after the first Saudi charities set up shop. It was designated by the US as a terror sponsor in 2008. In the meantime, it went through several name changes and permutations in both Kosovo and Albania, just like Al Haramain. Albania closed it down in 2004, but Kosovo did not do so until more than a decade later.

The SJRC was very ambitious, at first. In 2000, it laid the foundation for a multimillion-dollar cultural, sports, and religious center in Pristina. But 9/11 put a stopper in such splashy projects. There were raids carried out across the Balkans in 2001 and 2002. In March 2002, Bosnian authorities seized a number of files related to Osama bin Laden and Al Qaeda at the Sarajevo office of the Benevolence International Foundation, a Saudi charity: meeting minutes, Afghanistan activity reports,

letters, maps. So SJRC stuck to its grassroots dawa. But even its
bread-and-butter religious initiatives were in constant friction
with an aggressively secular new state. There is a strong tradition of secular government in the Albanian world, and even
today, Kosovo does not, for instance, allow female students to
wear the hijab in a country that is 95 percent Muslim.

Keep in mind that, in the bigger picture, the single most
influential foreign power during this time in Kosovo was the US,
the country that spearheaded an unprecedented NATO campaign without UN endorsement in service of a small, landlocked
nation's bid for independence. Even today, USAID placards are
ubiquitous across Kosovo and in Pristina there is a "Ričard Hol-
bruk" Street, a huge statue of Bill Clinton with comically large
hands, and a "Hillary" [Clinton] pantsuit boutique.

Some in Kosovo see US and Saudi efforts in their country
as complementary, despite their nominally opposed outcomes,
due to the well-known partnership between the two countries. "Where America is strong, Wahhabism is also strong,"
said Osman Musliu, an imam in central Kosovo. And the Saudi
investments often filled in gaps in the places where UN and
Western aid did not reach. What distinguished Saudi aid from
the rest was that missionary activity went hand in hand with
its charity.

The New Salafis
The most powerful legacy of Saudi dawa in Kosovo is the
group of Saudi-educated imams who have become hugely popular in the postwar era. Not all of them are Salafis: in fact, a
vocal minority of Saudi alumni are stridently anti-Salafi. For

148   instance, a Medina alumnus in the former camp is Dr. Shefchet
       Krasniqi, one of the most popular Salafi imams in Kosovo. He
       was classmates in Medina with the Podujevo imam Idriz Bilali,
       who was ousted from his post for being a critic of Salafi inroads.

       Having started in the Yugoslav era through the Islamic
       University of Medina, Saudi scholarships greatly increased in
       number after the war. No wonder, then, that a solid Salafi move-
       ment emerged in Kosovo within just a few years.

       "At this point, Saudis invest more in people than in new
       mosques and schools," said Skender Preteshi, of the Kosovo
       Center for Security Studies, a think tank in Pristina. "The most
       influential Saudi project is the people who study there and come
       back to Kosovo and become imams through the Islamic Com-
       munity here . . . Salafis are the ones in Kosovo with PhDs, mas-
       ter's degrees, and generally a lot of knowledge." A clutch of Salafi
       imams rose to the forefront in the new millennium, with many
       Saudi alumni among them: Enis Rama, Enes Goga, Mazlam
       Mazllami, Ekrem Afdiu, Fadil Sogujeva, Shefqet Krasniqi. Most
       of them studied in Saudi Arabia although a few, like Mazllami,
       studied in Cairo. Krasniqi, Sogujeva, and Goga all studied in
       Medina and Riyadh. Ekrem Afdiu, now a prominent preacher
       based in Mitrovica, once led an Islamic fighters unit in the KLA
       called "Abu Bekir Sidik," which included alumni of the Bosnian
       mujahideen. Mazllami, a radical imam in Prizren, is known for
       his anti-LGBT sermons and Enes Goga for advocating violence
       against Christians.

       The young Kosovars who became foreign fighters in ISIS
       are typically the counterpart of these Saudi-educated scholars,
       according to Preteshi. "They have less religious knowledge, so
       they are more impressionable," he said. He estimates, based on

fieldwork, that only 30 percent of foreign fighters were from
religious families, and the rest were from secular ones.

Because this new class of Salafi clerics emerged so suddenly, tensions ran high as soon as they started coming home.
And they immediately attracted both acolytes and detractors.
The atmosphere of the postwar religious revival was captured
by a Salafi-sympathetic Kosovar doctor who wrote an open
letter in 2003 arguing that the Islamic Community of Kosovo's
resistance to Salafism "betrayed their improper knowledge of
true Islam." A schism emerged between traditionalist and Salafi
factions amid the general Islamic revival, and outspoken members of the former camp were sometimes physically attacked.

In late 2008, Osman Musliu was appointed as the imam of
the main mosque in Drenas, in central Kosovo. But "the 'beards'
did not accept it," he said, referring to the Salafis who had
become numerous in the town. They had unsuccessfully nomi-
nated their own candidate for imam. On January 9, 2009, more
than a dozen Wahhabis from all around Kosovo and Macedonia
came in vans and attacked him in the mosque itself. Police eventually broke it up and sentenced the attackers to three months
in jail, but not before Osman got a black eye and a broken arm.
Later, he admitted, he went and beat up the opposition candidate himself, named Mehmeti Gazmend, who still preaches in a
rival mosque in Drenas.

Musliu says he was courted, like all imams in Kosovo after
the war, by Saudi Arabia; the Joint Relief Commission gave
most of them $200 a month in envelopes to encourage their
preaching. He managed to retain it only for a two-month trial
period in 1999, although the funding only continued for sympathetic imams, which he clearly was not. "They only kept them

up for people who were considered loyal," he said. He claims that the process helped them register all the imams in Kosovo and identify key players to support. Like many Kosovars, he believes that people got discreet cash payments after the war for growing out their beards or wearing hijabs, a phenomenon also reported in postwar Bosnia. He himself has a trimmed salt and pepper beard, and a deeply lined face.

His anti-Salafi screeds made little impact in the general discourse until the ISIS foreign fighter phenomenon began in earnest and the country switched gears into a counterextremist moral panic. People started to tell him, "If we had paid more attention to you, maybe this wouldn't have happened." He is critical of the Grand Mufti (chief cleric) of Kosovo, Naim Ternava, who was already in his post during his attack a decade ago, and whom he calls overly sympathetic to Wahhabi elements in the nation's religious life. Ternava has been continuously elected as Grand Mufti since 2003.

Musliu is not the only one who has criticized Ternava along these lines. Zenun Pajasiti, the former Interior Minister and a current MP, said that the Interior Ministry flagged numerous Saudi religious investments in 2008 and 2009, right after Kosovo declared its independence. He conveyed this to Ternava at the time, but the Grand Mufti was not interested in taking a closer look. Pajasiti considered it "very bad news" that Ternava was reelected in 2018. Idris Bilali, in Podujevo, said the Islamic Community "offered up its whole infrastructure to Salafi ideas."

Another traditional Muslim figure who was attacked by Wahhabis is Xhabir Hamiti, a theology professor at the University of Pristina who, ironically, also studied in Medina for five years but became a prominent critic of Salafism in Kosovo.

(His trajectory recalls that of Ulil Abshar-Abdalla in Jakarta who made a similar whiplash turn from a Saudi university to anti-Salafism.) Hamiti wrote an op-ed warning about rising fundamentalism in Kosovo and was brutally attacked by Salafis on November 30, 2008, shortly after Kosovo declared its independence. No one was arrested in connection with the crime.

Hamiti studied in Medina as a citizen of Yugoslavia from 1988 to 1993, getting a bachelor's and master's degree before going onward to Jordan and then Sarajevo for his PhD. An IUM delegation came to the Balkans and recruited him from the Alauddin Madrasa, the most prominent Islamic secondary school in Kosovo. The university was still fairly cosmopolitan, and his Arabic professor, for instance, was from India. But he was embarrassed to learn in his classes that many of the religious traditions he grew up with, like visiting tombs and even the way he stood to pray, were strongly discouraged or labeled as polytheistic.

Hamiti had become a young professor in Pristina when the war ended in 1999 and he recoiled at the influx of Saudi NGOs like Al-Haramain, having spent years in the heartland of Wahhabism. "Their CDs, cassettes, books—they were everywhere," he said. "Translated so quickly into Albanian. Not just in mosques but also in malls and the plazas. They even knocked on my door to proselytize!" Since 1999, he has collected the various different Salafi books that made their way to Kosovo. Today, the number is over 250 and he hopes to categorically index them soon.

Many of his graduate students in Pristina today are IUM alumni. Hamiti says they are distinguished in the classroom by a fixation on the Hadith, the sayings and doings of the Prophet.

152   These young scholars are often more dour than combative. "I try
to joke with them that the Prophet didn't want you to cut your
trousers short in a cold country like Kosovo," he said, referring to a popular sartorial Salafi affectation. But it doesn't get
a laugh.

Rebel Imams

When Xhabir Hamiti and other Yugoslav students studied in Medina in the 1980s and 1990s, they were taught by Indians, Egyptians, Jordanians, and Sudanese professors. The university was a microcosm of the ambitious, global, multicultural Saudi dawa project. By the time Drilon Gashi, a young Kosovar imam, arrived there in 2007, the university staff were mostly Saudis. In the late 1990s, IUM became strained from the tensions between the apolitical literalist scholars and the international Muslim Brotherhood activists who shared its roof. Its international phase came to a close, ceding to a house brand of apolitical Salafism that emphasized subservience to the state.

Gashi lives in Peja, a small city in western Kosovo that seems even smaller against its imposing backdrop of the slate-gray Accursed Mountains. Now thirty-three, he grew up in Istog and was educated, like Hamiti, at the Alauddin Madrasa in Pristina. He was a student there when the war ended and saw Saudi missionaries flood the school with Salafi books and pamphlets. They stoked his curiosity to study in their country and

154   he won a scholarship to the Islamic University of Medina, where he studied sharia as an undergraduate. There were no elective courses and he and all his coursemates were taught from a rigid standard curriculum.

At first, Gashi was thrilled. He had been unimpressed with the opportunities for a young Muslim scholar in Kosovo, where, in his words, the imams are more interested in worldly affairs than the Quran and engage in blind imitation (*taqlid*) of tradition instead of real scholarship. "After the war, it seemed like the Saudis were the only ones with real knowledge," he said. We met at a large, empty strip-mall restaurant on a brilliant autumn morning in Peja, before his weekly Friday sermon. He had dark circles under his eyes and dark gelled hair and wore a pilled blue sweater under a brown suit.

He lived in Medina with his wife, also a Kosovar, and had a monthly scholarship of two hundred euros. They were given a free apartment and he earned even more on the side by going on "proxy pilgrimage" (*hajj al-badal*) for elderly or sick Kosovars who could not make it to Mecca and Medina. "We used to have quite a lot of money," he said, bluntly. He was visited several times there by Sabahuddin Selmani, a Macedonian Salafi scholar who obtained a PhD in Medina, stayed in Saudi Arabia to work in its Ministry of Education, and is now considered to be a "godfather" of the modern Albanian Salafi community for his work recruiting students from the Balkans.

"Every time he visited me, he gave me two hundred euros to go back to Kosovo and spread the Salafi movement, because I was a good student," he said. "At least at first." Gashi says he really "loved" the Wahhabi ideology when he landed at IUM and he quickly memorized the Ibn Abd al-Wahhab texts he was

assigned there. "I used to know them inside out. He was seen as
a 'superman' of theology there."

But Gashi inherited from his father, also an imam, an
instinct for self-study that drove him to the library once he
plowed through the standard Salafi canon. He began to have
doubts about the work of Ibn Taymiyya, the austere medieval
theologian who is a tentpole of the Salafi and Wahhabi canons.
He started to ask questions in lectures, which were not enter-
tained, and he would trail his professors to their cars to follow
up. He also struggled to believe specific Wahhabi doctrines like
that God is an anthropomorphic figure in Heaven. He read more
widely outside his syllabus and wrote the names of Sufi and liberal theologians on his classrooms' blackboards to encourage
his classmates to do the same. That really got him in hot water.

"They told me to either get in line or get kicked out," he said.
"I didn't want to lose my scholarship so I stayed, suppressed my
questions, and got my degree."

It is interesting that, across the Muslim world, a considerable fraction of students who study in immersive Wahhabi
environments end up rejecting the approach wholesale. Anec-
dotally, IUM is known to have high drop-out rates, due in part to
the challenge of accepting its orthodoxy, according to Michael
Farquhar, who wrote a history of the university. Gashi couldn't
countenance staying a day longer in Saudi Arabia after his bachelor's degree so he got his master's degree in Jordan and finally
moved back to Kosovo in 2015, where the Islamic Community
assigned him to be an imam of a new mosque in Peja.

The mosque, Xhamia e Dritës ("Mosque of Light") was built
with funding from the UAE and it is bright, drywall-white with
prefab gray domes. When I visited, Gashi deposited me on the

empty second floor, where I was eye-level with a cone-shaped candelabra. Gashi emerged after a few minutes onto a small pulpit in resplendent Balkan Islamic dress, a loose suit in heavy black cloth and a red-and-white fez. He directed the assembly of men—they were all men, mostly in jeans and track pants—on the ground floor in prayer and then gave a brisk sermon in Albanian about the importance of play, personal inquiry, and enjoying life. The closing line was: "If you don't enjoy life here, you won't enjoy the afterlife." It seemed like a pointed rebuke of the Wahhabism that he had grown to despise.

Since returning to Kosovo, Gashi has been cataloguing what he considers to be the ceaseless Wahhabi and Salafi inroads on the country's Muslims. After the Friday sermon, in his small office that is attached to the mosque, he took off his hat and robes and pulled out stacks of the Salafi books in Albanian that had made their way into Peja in recent years. One was an Albanian translation of *Love and Hate in Islam* by Shaykh Muhammad Saeed Al-Qahtani; the title refers to the Salafi concept of *al-wala' wa-l-bara*—to love what Allah loves and hate what Allah hates. (This concept is typically used to brand non-Salafis as unbelievers or polytheists and is one of the key tenets of twenty-first-century Salafi-jihadism.) The volume was printed in Skopje in 2016 and edited by Sabri Bajgora of the Islamic Community of Kosovo. The NUN publishing house in Macedonia, established in 1999, is one of the key publishers of Albanian-language Salafi books, said Gashi, as is the Kalem publishing house in Pristina. There were stacks of other hard- and soft-cover books, as well as slim pamphlets on "Teuhidit" (Albanian for tawhid) and "Selefizmit" (Salafism) by "Ibën Baz" (Bin Baz) and "Abdul Vehabi" (Ibn Abd al-Wahhab). One even dated to before the war, an Albanian-language book of Bin Baz's lecture *There Is No God but Allah* that was printed in 1995, in the northern Kosovo town of Mitrovica.

Gashi's partner in this undertaking is another Peja-based imam, Zuhdi Hajzeri, age thirty-three. Hajzeri is not merely very tall, at over 6 foot 4, but somehow stretched out, with long fingers and an angular face set off by rimless, usually skewed rectangular glasses. Hajzeri's father and grandfather were both imams. He studied theology at Al-Azhar in Cairo and returned to Peja in 2010 to preach at the Taftali mosque, which dates back to 1587. (Its name comes from the Turkish word *taft,* meaning wood.) When Gashi moved to Peja, Hajzeri immediately recognized him as a fellow skeptic and they became fast friends. Their friendship centers on a Sisyphean effort to catalog Salafism in their midst and push for reform in the Islamic Community. "I'm the books guy," said Gashi, at one point, "and he's the institutions guy."

Peja was one of the places most damaged by the Kosovo War: every one of its forty-nine Islamic sites, including thirty-six mosques, as well as schools, a Turkish bath, and a library, was attacked by Serbs in 1998 and 1999. In fall 2018, when I visited for the first time, Peja's streets were covered in an inch of yellow leaves. In the harsh sunlight, it seemed exposed. Gashi and I went to visit Hajzeri at home. He had just had hip surgery and opened the door with some effort. His house was heated by a huge, tubular, stand-alone fireplace that rendered the living room like an oven. His elderly mother came in periodically to feed it more logs.

In rapid-fire, excitable speech, taking turns to pull up files both digital and in folders, Gashi and Hajzeri showed their collected photos and documents of Salafi preachers in Kosovo who maintain connections to the Gulf. They each had a bit of the red-string conspiracy theorist, but their curation of digital errata was nonetheless compelling. Among their data were items like: a photo of Enes Goga with Husain Sarraj, the Iraqi leader of the Al Waqf Al Islami NGO, at a Ramadan iftar; photos of the four mosques in Peja that were built with Saudi funding; Enes Goga's stack of letters to the Islamic Community of Kosovo attacking Gashi for supporting Darwin's theory of evolution; photos of the charitable activities of an NGO called Pema E Bamiresise, or the Tree of Mercy, which was forced to close due to its Gulf links; a photo of a Salafi preacher from Podujevo, Fadil Musliu, attending a training course in Saudi Arabia; photos of Behar Beqiri, a former classmate of Gashi's from Medina who now resells Saudi dates in Kosovo and posts anti-LGBT and anti-Jewish tirades on Facebook; a photo of the Kosovar Salafi preacher Enis Rama with Amroz Berisha, an Albanian-German cleric, in Saudi Arabia; a photo of a Salafi cleric protesting against the government's 2010 ruling that bans female students from wearing a headscarf in schools; photos from the regular Saudi pilgrimage trips from Peja led by Ernes Goga, a Salafi preacher and younger brother of the prominent Salafi imam Enes Goga.

Most of these were gathered from social media and a few from private messages sent by fellow travelers. The sum total of their work left the impression not of some kind of Salafi takeover of Kosovo, but the obvious fact that many Salafi imams in Kosovo today maintain active and extensive ties with the Gulf. Hajzeri grabbed a cushion to pad his chair, in obvious pain, and went on.

"It's not that Saudis have a monopoly on hardline Islam," he said. His own college roommate in Egypt was Sadullah Bajrami, now a prominent hardline Macedonian Salafi. And of course Gashi himself studied in Medina. "It's not illegal," said Hazjeri, to be Salafi. "We just want to stake our position outside of it, since there seems to be no strong opposition to it."

Hajzeri and Gashi's work seemed marginal at best until August 2014, which Burim Ramadani of the Interior Ministry pinpointed as a turning point for the conversation on extremism in Kosovo. That was when police indicted fifty-one people in an anti-extremism roundup, including over a dozen imams. Overnight, it seemed as though the state had mainstreamed the concerns of Hajzeri and Gashi.

War Panic

In 2016, a cache of ISIS registration documents, dubbed "*mujaheed* data," leaked out of Raqqa. They were the questionnaires that new foreign fighters had to fill out when they showed up at the Islamic State. They answered nearly two dozen questions about their background, including a self-reported assessment of their religious knowledge—"basic," "average," or "high." All six of the Kosovars represented in the leak professed that their knowledge was "basic." Also, none of the six fighters had gone to college, nor had any of them had a stable job, taking instead gig work in Kosovo in areas like butchery and construction. One foreign fighter who spent a month in Syria in 2013 said that Lavdrim Muhaxeri, the infamous Kosovar commander, preferred "obedient" recruits to highly educated, religiously convicted ones, and specifically asked the radical imam Zekirija Qazimi to send him more of the former.

This snapshot into Kosovar ISIS recruits illustrates the complexity of the moral panic that gripped Kosovo in 2014. At least a few of these foreign fighters were not going out of major theological conviction in Salafi-jihadism, but out of an inchoate desire to fight alongside their "Muslim brothers" against Bashar al-Assad. Over the past two decades, many Kosovars had realized for the first time that they were part of a global *umma,* the community of Muslim believers. Their politicians, up until 2012, and mainstream media, broadcast nonstop coverage of the Syrian War. And many of them, like the fighters recorded in the mujaheed data, had nothing really going for them at home. So they left.

About four hundred foreign fighters went from Kosovo to Syria between 2012–2016. Three-quarters of them were young people between the ages of seventeen and thirty. It is the foreign fighter phenomenon that has drawn Salafism in Kosovo into the spotlight in recent years.

Albert Berisha, one of the most famous returned foreign fighters, was a promising young political scientist applying for a PhD when he, by his own admission, decided to go to Syria at age twenty-six for "humanitarian reasons," to fight Assad. "I did not leave because I was desperate," he said, in a televised interview. "And [I] can't deny the role of religion. Sacrificing oneself to protect someone who is defenseless is a noble cause." He was disillusioned when he got there and left in less than ten days. His lawyer, Hedije Ademi, later told me, "The first time I met him, I yelled at him, 'Why the hell did you go there?'" She said he was intelligent, remorseful, and even set up an NGO to prevent more young people from immigrating there, although he eventually got a three-year jail sentence in 2018. "In my opinion, many young people like him feel sympathy for Syrians because they, too, experienced a war," she said. "And for a long time, our politicians here were playing a dangerous game, because they went on and on about the humanitarian crisis there."

Another young Kosovar who traveled to Syria in 2013 said, speaking anonymously, "When the Arab Spring began, I wanted to help the Syrian people. I have experienced war and horrific raids firsthand as a child in Kosovo, and wanted to help those children, the families."

Even Lavdrim Muhaxeri, the Albanian ISIS commander, went to Syria in 2012, before ISIS even existed. (Though he later took to the caliphate with great zeal.) The first Kosovar to be reported killed in Syria was a KLA veteran who died in November 2012, also well before ISIS.

None of this is meant to exculpate religious ideology. In one analysis of 142 foreign fighters, there was no measurable correlation between poverty or unemployment and going to Syria. "If it were just socioeconomic, all of Kosovo's Roma [the itinerant people sometimes called gypsies] would be in Syria now," said Albanian-American security analyst Adrian Shtuni, who conducted the survey. Ideology is the obvious remaining factor. At least one Kosovar foreign fighter, Valon Musliu, studied in Saudi Arabia. Eight of the eleven imams in Kosovo arrested between August and September 2014 on charges of preaching extremism were educated in the Gulf or Egypt. The Albanian imam Genci Balla, now thirty-nine, studied at the Islamic University of Medina and was arrested in 2014 in Tirana on charges of recruiting "dozens" of fighters to Syria. The ethnic Albanian foreign fighters were the visible tip of "an extensive network of like-minded militants, supporters, and enablers who not only

162   share the same ideology but are also actively engaged in its dissemination and recruitment efforts through physical and virtual social networks," according to a report by Shtuni. That is to say, extremism had reached a wide enough base by 2013, in less than two decades, that when the opportunity of fighting in Syria arose, there were plenty of willing ears.

Some of the imams under fire straddled precisely the same fine line as Saudi Arabia itself, between quietist Salafism and its violent applications. Enis Rama, a prominent Saudi-educated imam in Mitrovica, was arrested in September 2014, but denounced violent extremism as unacceptable earlier that year. Shefchet Krasniqi, another prominent Salafi imam, denounced Lavdrim Muhaxeri by name. One foreign fighter from the town of Ferizaj went to Syria despite the majority opinion of imams in Kosovo, whom he described as "swingers." "They tell you something one day, something else another day, this and that, and they are cowards." At least one jihadist professed that he had been *de*-radicalized by listening to the nonviolent Salafi teachings of Enis Rama and Ekrem Afdiu.

Mosques that hosted Salafi preachers were undoubtedly significant to the foreign fighter phenomenon too, and Saudi Arabia financed dozens of them. The mere coincidental proximity to a Salafi mosque has on several occasions turned Kosovars into foreign fighters. One young man in Pristina decided to become a more pious Muslim in his twenties and went to the nearest mosque, which happened to be the Dardanija mosque, once home to the Saudi Joint Relief Committee headquarters. The majority of congregants there were of Salafi persuasion— and the radical imam Rexhep Memishi had an office nearby—so he, too, became swept up in it and went to Syria in 2013.

Some of the most radical Salafi-jihadist views were propagated by foreign-educated Albanian imams in Skopje, Macedonia. Two radical imams, Shukri Aliu (born in Kosovo) and Rexhep Memishi (born in Macedonia) both studied briefly at the Islamic University of Medina, but were both actually thrown out of there for being *too* radical. Both found more Salafi-jihadist fellow-travelers instead in Egypt, as well safe havens to live and spread their teachings in Kosovo in the mid-2000s. Shukri Aliu influenced both Zekirija Qazimi, a Kosovar imam who explicitly supported Salafi-jihadism and sent followers to Lavdrim Muhaxeri, and Ridvan Hafiqi, an influential Kosovar foreign fighter who became an ISIS commander. Aliu was probably the most influential propagator of Salafi-jihadism in southern Kosovo, and the villages around his hometown contributed a disproportionate number of foreign fighters to Syria. He was eventually extradited from Kosovo and imprisoned in Macedonia. The Albanian Genci Balla, the most prolific foreign fighter recruiter, of about seventy men, studied at IUM, too, and was sentenced to seventeen years in jail in 2016.

There were even dormitories for young Salafi-jihadists in downtown Pristina, dubbed "Muhaxeri's Quarter," after Lavdrim Muhaxeri. Muhaxeri himself was a highly modern kind of jihadist; he was known to rush home from the battlefield to check how much his Facebook videos were liked and shared.

The Syrian War produced distinct opportunities for religious leaders, according to the Kosovar-British political scientist Behar Sadriu. It gave them unprecedented media coverage and an increased viewership for their online material, which can be traced in the spikes in their viewership in 2014. The Salafi corpus seeded over the last two decades was ripe for rediscovery.

Four municipalities of Kosovo near the Macedonian border were disproportionately represented and accounted for about a third of all foreign fighters. Southern Kosovo and northwestern Macedonia, accordingly, were major targets of Gulf charity after the war. They tend to be less developed than the metropolitan regions around Pristina. Macedonia, where Albanian Muslims are a minority and which fought its own war in 2001 and 2002, also became something of a Salafi stronghold. Salafi-jihadists maintained a cross-border jihadi recruitment camp between Jažince in northern Macedonia and Kaçanik in Kosovo. One ISIS recruit who did not end up going to Syria attended sermons organized by a charity in Kaçanik called Islamic Youth where he attended a series of progressively more conservative sermons, starting with why men should not shake hands or socialize with women gradually transitioning into the duty to fight in Syria. A member of the Kosovo national police confirmed to me the existence of more short camps, lasting three to seven days, for secondary school kids in the small town of Prevala, near Prizren, from which some people did eventually become foreign fighters.

I visited two of these small towns, Elez Han and Kaçanik, in late 2018. Together, they contributed thirty fighters to Syria, most of whom were now in jail. To put this in perspective, Elez Han's foreign fighter rate was five times as high as that of the Belgian suburb of Molenbeek, which is infamously one of the jihadist hotbeds of Europe. Kaçanik was also the hometown of the commander Lavdrim Muhaxeri.

Although Kaçanik is tiny, it contained all the building blocks of a small Kosovar town: in front of its municipal building was a placard advertising USAID's "Democratic Effective Municipalities" program and behind it was a small, Ottoman-style mosque. Old men in thick wool caps paced up and down the main street. The municipal building had no elevators and a linoleum-padded stairwell. The mayor of Kaçanik, Besim Ilazi, is a KLA veteran and has been elected for three successive terms since 2012. His office was festooned with statues of Albanian eagles and KLA paraphernalia. Twenty-two people from his town immigrated to Syria; he seemed befuddled by the whole affair, even four years later, and suggested that social media amplified the pull of Syrian conflict. "It was proclaimed that Syria was going through a violent crisis, much like our own in Kosovo, and our guys who went over there wanted to put down Assad," he said. He also confirmed that there had been terrorist training camps in the nearby town of Vitia.

There were no imams apprehended in Kaçanik, but he suspected that geography played a role in the townspeople's radicalization. "The closer to Skopje [the capital of Macedonia], the more religious, is how people are in Kosovo," he said. Many people have familial links across the border, too. He himself never prays and sees the foreign fighter phenomenon as an enigma. He repeatedly suggested that the best way to fight extremism would be to have more sports teams for young people.

From there I drove to Elez Han, another small town that was home to eleven foreign fighters. Its name means "shelter" and it used to be known for its lodges for traders passing through the valley. In the car, I listened to a protest song, by a heavy metal band called Troja, railing against the Kosovar diaspora. They screamed, "Bring us knowledge, no more cars!" I wondered how the residents of these small wayside towns in Kosovo felt about their relatives who had escaped into the diaspora, who could travel without a visa into places that did not even recognize Kosovo as a country.

The municipal office of Elez Han had even more KLA para-phernalia and somehow, despite the incipient winter, a variety of thriving hothouse plants. There was a photo of factory smokestacks in a gold frame and a few swords were mounted on the walls. The mayor, Rufki Suma, had a talk show silently playing on the TV in his office and summoned a male atten-dant to bring him a notebook so that he could take his own notes during our interview. He, too, is a KLA veteran and became the first and only mayor of Elez Han in 2009, when the town broke away from Kaçanik. He, too, lamented the loss of the town's only soccer field. Ten of the foreign fighters from his town, all male, have returned to Kosovo and five are already free. One of them is back in civil society making handicrafts. "He needs machines to scale up his business, but I can't give it to him," said Suma, who criticized the narrow vision of what constitutes counterex-tremism activities from UN and US funders.

There has been a sort of generational whiplash in how fast all of this transpired. One intelligence officer in Kaçanik described several cases where fathers who had been atheists or hardline Communists in pre-independence Kosovo found that their sons had become Salafi Muslims or jihadists. Kosovo is a small country and everyone knows someone who has been or tried to go to Syria. Burim Ramadani, of the Defense Min-istry, was deeply affected by some of the stories of emigration and is writing a novel about a pair of brothers he met in "one of the small towns in Macedonia" who went separate ways after their father died. One left Kosovo to seek work in Germany and the other fell in with radical imams, went to Syria, and died in combat. "It's a perfect story," he joked, "because those are the two most attractive paths for our young people."

The Roundup

In the summer of 2014, alarmed by the immigrations to Syria, Kosovar authorities rounded up fifteen imams. They included Zekirija Qazimi, the notorious recruiter for Muhaxeri, whom authorities said was funded by Gulf charities, and other prominent imams with huge followings including Enes Goga from Peja, Idriz Biliani and Mazllam Mazllami from Prizren, and Enis Rama, Bedri Robaj, and Shefqet Krasniqi from Pristina. Their charges include financing terrorism, inciting ethnic and religious hatred and intolerance, recruiting militants, and encouraging people to immigrate to Syria. Only Qazimi was actually jailed, for ten years, after he was found hiding in a forest. But the rest of the Kosovar imams were detained and released.

It was a swift and impressive crackdown for a small country whose counterterrorism directorate was only established in 2007. In 2015, Kosovo passed a law prohibiting foreign fighters from leaving the country. In the last three years, the Kosovo police claim to have prevented four planned domestic terror attacks, arrested forty people planning to go to Syria, arrested more than two hundred returning foreign fighters, and closed more than twenty charities.

But the crackdown has also been wielded as a blunt instrument. Only one of the Kosovo imams, Zekirija Qazimi, actually went to jail. The rest of the imams, who were detained and subsequently released, see the ordeal as evidence of their courage under a fundamentally anti-religious state. Although they have now toned down or eliminated their Syria rhetoric, nearly all are still committed Salafis.

I met two of the most prominent Saudi-educated imams who were detained and then released in the crackdown, Enes Goga and Ekrem Afdiu. Their stories perfectly illustrate the tension between conservative but nonviolent Salafism and problematic offshoots of Salafi-jihadism in Kosovo. It's not clear that "cracking down" on the former is at all productive in addressing the latter, mirroring the dilemma faced by Saudi Arabia itself. I met Goga in Peja, the same city where Gashi and Hajzeri live and where Goga is the head imam, at a sprawling restaurant off the main square. The city's downtown was an unmixed salad of aesthetics: a looming Yugoslav-era hotel on one side, a tiny postwar "Friendship Park" on the other. Goga shook my hand heartily when he walked in, which was a surprise, given my experience with Salafis in Southeast Asia, who would never do such a thing. Goga is now forty-one and is the eighth imam in his family; his younger brother and cousin are the ninth and tenth. His grandfather was a *hafiz* who memorized the Quran, and his father was an imam, too.

Goga was born and raised in Peja. In the 1980s, he was a student of Imam Rexhep Morina, one of the first Salafi imams in Kosovo, who left before the war and now lives in Illinois. He studied at the Alauddin Madrasa from 1994 to 1997, studied Arabic in Jordan for nine months, and then went to the Islamic University of Medina in 1997. His studies were interrupted by the war, so he came home in 1998 to fight with the Kosovo Liberation Army and returned to Medina after the cease-fire in 1999. He studied sharia there and graduated in 2003. He spoke admiringly of the international atmosphere in Medina, where he was friends with people like a white American Muslim convert and his African-American wife. "But I was jealous of their US passports!" he said. "I only have this awful Kosovo one." He also claimed that Kosovars were the best Arabic speakers there, and credited his prowess to the superior "syntax and morphology" he learned at the Pristina madrasa.

He was quickly hired as an imam back in his hometown and his stature grew steadily until 2009, when he became the head of the Islamic Community of Peja. The only hiccup came in 2014, when he was arrested under suspicion of terrorism and promoting hate speech, but was detained for fifteen days and then released. He went to trial in 2017 for the hate speech charge— the terrorism charge was dropped—and after twelve court sessions, was ruled innocent.

Why had he been arrested? "When a director wants a good movie, he needs great actors," he said. "When I and my colleagues were arrested, we seemed like good actors." He admitted that he had spoken out often against the Assad regime in Syria but claimed that the rise of ISIS on social media was a parallel phenomenon that he did not endorse. He also claimed that the real extremists were in Macedonia, where he has lectured in the past, and said that they spread their ideology in Kosovo between 2002 and 2010. His added that his wife is an endocrinologist and neither of his sons attends a madrasa, by way of bolstering his secular credentials.

Drilon Gashi said Goga once delivered a guest lecture in his mosque asserting that they would bring the headscarf and sharia into Kosovo, by force if needed. Hajzeri also debated Goga in 2013 about the jihad in Syria; Goga claimed it was a legitimate

170 cause at the time and Hajzeri did not. Gashi had also showed me a light blue pamphlet of Enes Goga's translation of the *Book of Tawhid*, the key Wahhabi text.

As for Saudi Arabia, Goga said "you don't learn extremism in the schools but in the streets." He went to the kingdom for hajj in 2010 and 2018 but otherwise says he is more interested in Europe than the Gulf. He proudly showed me photos of seminars he has held at the Finsbury Park mosque in London and bragged that Nazir Ahmed, a Kashmiri-British life peer in the House of Lords, had visited him in Peja.

Goga feels vindicated by the results of his trial, but also vindictive. He rattled off the names of journalists whom he said had "lynched" him with "fake news." It's hard not to think that the highly tenuous arrest of a conservative imam like Goga was anything more than a desperate reaction to a crisis that a young country like Kosovo was in no position to handle.

Kosovo's problem is not with radicalism but with a lack of opportunities, said Goga. He looked at me pointedly and said, "If you were born in Bombay you would have had fewer opportunities than you did as an American. Isn't it true?" I said, probably, yes. After all, I did not even have to apply for a visa to visit Kosovo. "It's the same in Kosovo."

I met the other detained imam, Ekrem Afdiu, shortly thereafter at Pristina's Grand Hotel, a thirteen-story, Yugoslav-era concrete behemoth where the dictator Josip Tito used to have a reserved suite. Afdiu had a wiry gray beard and wore a huge onyx ring, and his left eye was half-closed in a squint. "I speak to you with an open heart," he said gravely, at the outset. Now he is forty-seven and based in Mitrovica, but he travels frequently to

Pristina to, among other things, deliver his regular program on the Salafi channel called Peace TV. He was actually on his way to the studio when we met and was wearing a dark suit for the occasion. He studied in Medina from 1990 to 1997, getting a BA and MA in Sunnah and Hadith studies. Even today, he said, anyone who wants to get a scholarship to Saudi Arabia can "easily" do so; he sometimes writes their letters of recommendation. He was nineteen when he first moved to Medina and admitted he knew little about Islam from his youth in Yugoslavia and learned "everything" in the kingdom. From 2001 to 2006, he lectured at a Saudi Joint Relief Committee mosque in Dardanija. Now he is at the Mosque Tamik in Mitrovica. Afdiu's NGO, called Gjurma, which translated several Salafi texts into Albanian, was closed in 2018 among the crackdown on Islamic charities.

His preaching is often banal, focusing on the typical Salafi concerns of dress, daily interactions and behavior, and the mechanics of prayer. Relatably, he professes that he loves Twitter and posts several times a day to his more than seven thousand followers. He even presents a TV program called *Beyond Tweeting* where he discusses Twitter activity from the past week and how to find meaning in life beyond social media. He was chastened by the 2014 roundup and said his sermons now emphasize religious harmony and minimizing social friction.

What the state is struggling to understand, he said, is that there's nothing wrong with being a Muslim, even a visible or conservative Muslim, in an independent Kosovo, and the larger phenomenon can't be collapsed into real social problems like extremism or jihadism. Before we parted ways, he said, "Whenever foreigners meet me, the first thing they ask me is about my

172 beard. They think this is extremism, too. And I say, well, if this makes you an extremist then you can become an extremist for two euros."

From War to Peace TV

Ekrem Afdiu is one of the most prominent Kosovar guests on Peace TV Albanian, a media outlet that set up shop in Pristina in 2009 and is one of the biggest signs of the foothold that Salafis now have in Kosovo. Peace TV is an international Salafi channel founded by the radical Indian televangelist Zakir Naik, a physician born in Mumbai who became known for his hard-line English-language sermons and who now lives in exile in Malaysia. It is telling that there is an Albanian Peace TV channel in the first place, because it points to the large audience for Salafi media across Kosovo, Albania, and Macedonia. Although it doesn't publish viewing statistics, Peace TV Albanian has over 80,000 likes on Facebook. And it's even more telling that, of all the Albanian-speaking countries, Peace TV found the most amenable home in Pristina. Peace TV used to have physical headquarters in the city's Sunny Hill neighborhood but now records its various programs in a rented studio through a production company called Albunion Media. It's headed by the Pristina-based Salafi imam Enis Rama, a Medina alumnus. It broadcasts shows for thirteen hours a day, and within the last year, there have been over fifty different hosts and guests. Most of its presenters are from Kosovo, although there are a few Albanians and Macedonians.

They include Sabri Bajgora of the Islamic Community of Kosovo; Enes Goga, who has a weekly Quran reading program on Monday evenings; and Ekrem Afdiu. In between religious talk shows and Quran recitation programs, Peace TV also shows a few uncannily animated children's programs. One of them, which I watched at Zyhdi Hajzeri's house in Peja, showed a young girl in a hijab learning how to pray, in a glitchy and vaguely unsettling CGI animation.

It's a remarkable and broad media platform for Salafism, which had almost zero followers in Kosovo just thirty years ago. It's not a Saudi project per se, although Zakir Naik has close ties with Saudi Arabia and was granted Saudi citizenship in 2017, shortly after he fled terrorism charges in India. (Naik was also awarded the annual King Faisal International Prize for Service to Islam in 2015 by Saudi king Salman bin Abdulaziz.) What Peace TV Albanian really shows is how the short, intense period of Saudi investment and scholarships created a genuine Salafi base there in record time—just like in Indonesia and Nigeria— one that now sustains programming in its own language. It's even more remarkable when you recall that, under Serb occupation, there were hardly any Albanian-language TV programs allowed in Kosovo—many people's roofs even today retain the old clunky satellite dishes that Kosovars would use to access TV from across the border.

Given that the majority of influential Salafis, including Enes Goga and Ekrem Afdiu, support the local school of Hanafi jurisprudence rather than the Hanbali school in Saudi Arabia, it seems likely that a localized Salafism will take root in Kosovo, too, just as it has in Indonesia, Nigeria, and many other countries with large Muslim populations.

Today, according to a database of foreign NGOs maintained by Kosovo's Ministry of the Interior, none of the seven charities from Saudi Arabia and Kuwait that registered after the war, as well as the Saudi-funded Al Waqf Al Islami, have a license to operate in the country anymore. "In Kosovo today, it's impossible to register an explicit religious charity, so if anyone in Saudi Arabia wants to send money, they use workarounds," said Skender Preteshi, the security analyst. Some charities have been remarkably persistent, to the point where closing them is like playing Whack-a-Mole: a Deobandi charity run by an exiled Kosovar, Xhemajl Duka, was closed, but it turned out that he repeatedly reentered Kosovo to visit the mosque and orphanage he had set up in the village of Marina and still receives money transfers from Britain.

Saudi scholarships continue too, not just to IUM but also to Imam Muhammad bin Saud University in Riyadh, Umm al-Qura University in Mecca, and Qassim University in Jeddah. There are at least eighty Kosovars now studying in Saudi Arabia, per Idris Bilali. In order to get a scholarship from a Saudi university, Kosovars need a letter of support from at least one licensed imam in Kosovo, said Hajzeri, who added that he himself would not be authorized to write such a letter due to his outspoken views. Typically, it's granted only to trusted imams like Enis Rama and Enes Goga who are endorsed by the Islamic Community of Kosovo. The letters are usually fielded by the Albanian Sabahuddin Selmani, a former member of the Bosnian mujahideen who now works in the Saudi Ministry of Education. Students at Saudi universities get a stipend of about 600 euros a month, which goes up to 1,000 euros a month for graduates and 1,500 euros a month for advanced degrees like a PhD, plus free plane tickets and lodging.

"For scholarships, the kingdom has its own mechanisms," said Sabri Bajgora of the Islamic Community of Kosovo, saying that the community doesn't regulate them, "and students immediately get scholarships upon enrolment."

Bajgora is hoping to slow the educational pipeline to Saudi Arabia, although he is heartened by Crown Prince Muhammad bin Salaman (MBS) and his rhetoric of cracking down on extremism. "We have signed an agreement with Al-Azhar [in Egypt] to send more of our students there and we provide ten scholarships a year," he said.

The Islamic community's headquarters were burned down by Serbs in 1999 but reopened a few years later in downtown Pristina. Bajgora, looking tired despite his neat suit, met me in his office, where we sat on pink couches overlooking the Faculty of Islamic Studies, a religious school built after the war. "We're trying everything," he said. Bajgora's deputy, who was present at our meeting, said that he himself was an IUM grad and said he didn't love the religious climate of Saudi Arabia. "But it was free, so . . ."

The crackdown on several of the Community's own imams was hard on them, admitted Bajgora. "We don't think they are really extremists, but their vocabulary was problematic." They still keep tabs on the ones who were arrested. Shefqet Krasniqi is no longer allowed to lecture at the Great Mosque. (Although when I was in Kosovo, he gave a live televised sermon on TV Dukagjini and has certainly not absented himself from the public sphere.) And in Prizren, Mazllam Mazllami, a hardline imam suspended in 2014, was back in his regular mosque as of 2019.

Bajgora is an alumnus of Al-Azhar, as is Naim Ternava, the Grand Mufti of Kosovo. They were among the small group of five Kosovar Al-Azhar alumni who rebuilt the Community almost from scratch in 1999. They had to be scrappy because there

176   weren't many religious scholars in the new nation. Even today, said Bajgora, there is a shortage of imams in this small country.

New Spheres of Influence

I met with a senior Kosovo police officer in February, two days before independence day. "I'm not sure what we're celebrating," he said, darkly. "We're not independent," he said, "Kosovo can't ever be immune to foreign influence."

As Kosovo joins the greater Muslim world, through the various mechanisms of globalization, it has opened itself up, like all small Muslim countries, to ever more bids for influence. There are many more Gulf actors there now. The Kuwaiti government, through its Tirana embassy, donated two million euros for orphanages in Kosovo, overseen by the ambassador of Kuwait to Albania. "We negotiate with governments now, not charities," said Lutfi Haziri, the mayor of Gjilan, where one of the orphanages is currently under construction. Kuwait's Society of the Revival of Islamic Heritage (RIHS) also gave a 286,000-euro donation to a charity in Kosovo, through its embassy in Tirana, in 2014. In May 2014, Naim Ternava signed a 1.5-million-euro deal with the UAE's Minister of Finance, Sheikh Hamdan bin Rashid Al Maktoum, to fund eight new mosques in Kosovo.

At the same time, ever since the 2014 counterextremism crackdown, Gulf money has become almost categorically controversial. It's not helped by their non-transparent finances and sometimes defensive posture. The Qatar Charity, for instance, runs a large educational and vocational training center in downtown Pristina called the Infinit Center. Once linked to Al Qaeda, it is now largely aboveground. After 9/11, it operated under an

Albanian name, the Maqbullia Association, but reopened officially as the Qatar Charity in 2003, with a present staff of twenty-six and a budget of three million euros. It no longer has a religious component to its aid and mainly supports orphanages and computer and language classes. Still, Mahmoud Abbas Shaker, the Egyptian head of Qatar Charity's Infinit Center in Kosovo, became angry when I asked him to explain the charity's name changes through the years. Despite living in Kosovo for eighteen years, Shaker speaks little Albanian and we conducted our interview in Arabic.

Kuwait, the UAE, and Qatar, by and large, are less ideologically motivated in their charity in Kosovo today than Saudi Arabia in the postwar era. They rarely give religious books with aid, for example.

But above all today, there's Turkey. Having largely ignored postwar relief in Kosovo, Turkey, under President Recep Erdoğan, is making an ambitious new bid for cultural ties with its former Ottoman territories. On the desk of many Kosovar imams, I saw three flags: Kosovo, Albania, and Turkey. Turkey is building Pristina's new central mosque after a six-year-long competition to decide who would design it; the winning plan, put forth by the Turkish Directorate of Religious Affairs, is inspired by the 16th-century Selimiye Mosque in Edirne, Turkey. It doesn't hurt that Turkey is one of the only countries Kosovars can go to without a visa. The Diyanet, Turkey's Supreme Religious Council, has an office in Kosovo (as well as ones in Bosnia, Macedonia, and Bulgaria) and often sends extra imams there during Ramadan. And since 2007, the Diyanet has taken over the organization of all Balkan Muslims' hajj pilgrimage, a role formerly executed by a variety of Salafi organizations. This is a highly significant development for Balkan Islam since the pilgrimage to Mecca is obligatory for all able-bodied Muslims.

There are more than 1,300 students from Kosovo studying in Turkey now with scholarships, according to the Diyanet, which far outstrips the eighty to ninety Kosovars who study annually in Saudi Arabia. The title of largest mosque in the Balkans will soon pass from Sarajevo's Saudi-built King Fahd Mosque to the Turkey-built Tirana Grand Mosque.

Unlike in Indonesia and Nigeria, there are very few Shia in Kosovo, and Iran's influence is negligible, although not nonexistent. In the historic southern city of Prizren, there is a small NGO called the Quran Foundation that is affiliated with Iran's Al-Mustafa International University and directed by Ikballe Huduti-Berisha, a Shia convert who has met with former president Mahmoud Ahmadinejad in Iran.

These new religious actors may actually be a positive development. One reason that Salafism caught fire in Kosovo in the early millennium was that there was nothing else competing with it. But as Kosovo becomes more connected with the greater Muslim world and its religious sphere becomes more crowded, the dust will likely settle. It will almost certainly still include these Salafis, but, as in Indonesia and Nigeria, they will find that there are natural limits to their expansion.

Many Calls

On the northwestern outskirts of Riyadh is a sand-colored, mud-brick complex that were once home to the original House of Saud. This old city, Diriyah, was the seat of the Saudi royals from 1744 to 1818. Its cool, dark interiors would have been a respite from a capital brutally situated in the heart of the peninsula, surrounded by desert for hundreds of miles. It was in one of these buildings, with their tiny triangular windows, that Muhammad ibn Abd al-Wahhab signed his fateful pact with the royal family, pledging his pious credentials in support of their expansionary vision.

Today a billboard outside Diriyah welcomes visitors to the "home of the first Saudi state." The mosque where Ibn Abd al-Wahhab used to preach will be a museum. The kingdom is hoping that visitors will find Abd al-Wahhab's story to be an interesting arc of history, rather than a blotch on Saudi Arabia's image abroad. At the entrance to "Historical Diriyah" is a park, with fake trees and fake grass.

180   Everywhere in Saudi Arabia today, the past is up for grabs. In
Jeddah, I was eagerly welcomed into the Khuzam Palace, which
was technically closed for renovations, when it was determined
that I was an American. "You have to see this!" said Muhammad,
a recent college graduate working there. I followed him to a room
in the back with sandy uprooted floors and stained-glass windows. "This is where Abdul Aziz opened Saudi for oil exploration," he said. "To your country!"

Telling their own story of modern Saudi Arabia will be a
challenge for a kingdom now known to many for the effects of
their proselytization abroad. To the Saudi government, which is
also setting up a Muhammad ibn Abd al-Wahhab research center
in Diriyah, there is a hope to reframe the austere preacher as a sort
of founding father. That will be hard to do when his unambig-
uous teachings on intolerance and excommunication are easily
accessible at bookshops and on websites. But the project hints
at the kingdom's goals for soft power in the coming century.

For the first time in a long time, the country is even
acknowledging its pre-Islamic past, shocking in light of the
countless Muslim heritage sites that Wahhabis once destroyed
in their own soil. Foreign research teams are excavating the ten
thousand-year-old rock art of the Arabian desert, although
anything that happened in Saudi Arabia before the seventh century is still lumped together under *jahiliyyah*, the age of ignorance, as the entire antiquities section is denoted in Riyadh's
National Museum.

It's interesting that Saudi Arabia wants to include Wahhabism in its new public face, rather than merely sidestep the issue.
Perhaps they hope to silo it into the past and thus diminish its

present power. The Saudi-Wahhabi pact has always evolved and faced challenges, and today it's by MBS, who, in rhetoric at least, wants not to care about this ancient power-sharing agreement. He has already taken some bold steps to test it. The Committee for the Promotion of Virtue and the Prevention of Vice is no longer allowed to arrest people; there are a few new scholars in its top clerical bodies and some of them even follow schools of jurisprudence outside the Wahhabi Hanbali school. But the country still runs on Islamic law and the clerics are in charge of major universities, mosques, and institutions. The Wahhabi clerics are still "the only organized social base outside the state," said Bernard Haykel, a professor of Near Eastern studies at Princeton and one of the most prominent observers of Saudi current events.

One thing that is certain is that Saudi dawa is entering a fascinating new phase as the kingdom tries to balance the duty of the Wahhabi call to Islam against how Wahhabism is instrumentalized for the kingdom's national project today. Its dawa outposts may be more malleable to these shifting goalposts than previously thought. When I visited LIPIA in Jakarta in 2019, I was surprised to find it blanketed in paraphernalia of Vision 2030, the flagship modernization program of MBS. The school had a new leader, Dr. Ghazi Abdul Aziz, had employed a dozen new female faculty, and even started up a football team. The atmosphere was palpably different and more relaxed than my previous visits in 2017 and 2018.

Ghazi told me in no uncertain terms: "We take Vision 2030 to heart in everything we do. We want the school to be more modern, open, and moderate." Perhaps the changes were

182   partially cosmetic, since Ibn Abd al-Wahhab and Ibn Taymiyya were still on the curriculum. But a cosmetic shift is not nothing. "Vision 2030 is not just for inside Saudi Arabia," said Ghazi. "It's part of what Saudis do everywhere in the world."

Vision 2030

In November 2017, MBS declared that he intended to revive a "moderate Islam open to the world and all religions" in Saudi Arabia. He added, "We won't waste thirty years of our life combating extremist thoughts; we will destroy them now and immediately." Officials at the Saudi Ministry of Religious Affairs have indicated that MBS has indeed diminished the resources dedicated to religious institutions in charge of exporting Saudi Islam abroad, although exact figures are unlikely to emerge. But despite his dramatic proclamation, MBS is not as far outside the Wahhabi fold as he seems.

"Is MBS still a Wahhabi? He's definitely a Wahhabi," said Bruce Riedel, who now directs the Brookings Intelligence Project in Washington, D.C. "His extreme anti-Shiism, exemplified by the war in Yemen and calling Iran's Ayatollah Khomeini 'Hitler,' resonates very positively with the Wahhabi clerical establishment. They're willing to accommodate some of his social reforms like entertainment, tourism, and women driving because they're happy with his foreign policy outside and his crackdown on Shia inside the kingdom." And with regards to the greater royal family, "No king in recent memory has been as virulently anti-Shia as Salman has been, both internally and externally," said Riedel. Intolerance of Muslim minorities, one of the worst global effects of Saudi proselytization, is unlikely to decrease with such forceful reinforcements from the kingdom.

There have been some interesting new figures, though, like Dr. Mohammed bin Abdul-Karim Al-Issa, the newest secretary-general of the Muslim World League, appointed in 2016. He has openly acknowledged the horrors of the Holocaust with Jews in New York—Holocaust denial is not unusual from Saudis—and has said that Salafism is "just an approach" and not the only approach to Islam. He speaks at conferences with panels like "Moderation in Islamic History and Jurisprudence Heritage," "Moderation Between Authenticity and Modernity," "Differences and the Culture of Moderation," and "Moderation and the Message of Civilized Communication."

It has been an awkward new tone, at times. Several US diplomatic officials told me he appears "coached" in public appearances. A Saudi lobby in D.C., the Saudi Arabian Public Relations Committee, arranged one of his major trips, paying $35,000 in 2018 to bring Al-Issa to the Museum of Jewish Heritage in New York and meet and greet State Department officials to explain how the Muslim World League promotes moderation. But, as one now-jailed Saudi intellectual said: "How can one take Muhammad Al-Issa's statements seriously when religious bookstores in Riyadh are full of books advocating the exact opposite?"

MBS's purported crackdown on hardline clerics has actually, in practice, been a crackdown on disobedient clerics, and many of the most intolerant Wahhabis remain ensconced in their offices. For instance, Saleh al-Fawzan, a strident anti-Shia ideologue, remains in good favor with MBS whereas the scholar Abdullah Almalki, who has spoken in favor of increased civil liberties for Saudis, was arrested in September 2017 and sent to a secret trial. Most of the clerics who have tried to think critically about Wahhabism itself, like the liberal scholar Hasan al-Maliki

184 and the charismatic reformist Salman al-ʿAwda, are in jail now, too. It is unlikely that any of the core tenets of Wahhabism that cause discord, like intolerance of minorities and a violent disregard for regional practices, will truly change.

The Big Business of Moderate Islam

In 2018, Malaysia closed the Saudi-backed King Salman Centre for International Peace in Kuala Lumpur, because "Saudi Arabia was not qualified to lead such a centre in view of its official doctrine of Wahhabism which they said inspired the IS [Islamic State] ideology." What was unusual is not that they closed the center, which has numerous counterparts around the world, but that they explicitly called out the paradox at the heart of Saudi counterextremism.

Saudi Arabia has created a sort of cottage industry out of countering violent extremism, or "CVE," in the post-9/11 era. The world is littered with Saudi-funded CVE: the Saudi Al-Sakinah online anti-radicalization initiative; the King Abdullah bin Abdul-Aziz International Center for Interreligious and Intercultural Dialogue in Riyadh; a 560-mosque counterextremism project in Bangladesh; the United Nations Counter-Terrorism Centre, founded with a $10 million Saudi endowment in 2011 and buttressed by a $100 million donation in 2014. Saudi king Abdullah pioneered interfaith efforts after 9/11, becoming the first-ever Saudi royal to meet the pope and sponsoring dialogues in places like Geneva and Connecticut. The Muslim World League holds regular interfaith conferences—from the "World Conference on Dialogue" in Madrid in July 2008 to "Islam, a Message of Mercy and Peace" in Moscow in March 2019—although Shia leaders are usually and pointedly not invited.

At the same time, the actual quality of Saudi intelligence on terrorism has been falling, ever since MBS ousted the former Saudi intelligence chief, Prince Muhammad bin Nayaf (MBN), who was known for his intensive cooperation with the US on security issues. Inside the kingdom, MBN used to lead a pretty luxurious counterextremism and jihadist rehabilitation center in Riyadh called the Mohamed bin Nayaf Center for Counseling and Care. It included structured debates with Islamic scholars, leisure facilities, and vocational training that were the envy of poor Saudis who sometimes wondered why ex-terrorists got more welfare than them. This in-house deradicalization program was one of the "most professional, comprehensive and successful" ones in the world and had treated three thousand people by 2012. But its fate is unclear in the new regime.

In terms of terror finance, a 2018 analysis from the Financial Action Task Force concluded that Saudi Arabia now has a "solid understanding of the money laundering and terrorist financing risks it faces," but its "financial intelligence unit is not able to conduct sophisticated financial analysis" and "the lack of suspicious transaction reports, in particular on suspected cases of terrorist financing, is a concern." The kingdom accepted 41 requests as of 2016 to designate suspicious individuals, and designated 150 more on its own, but those listings are not public.

After the rise of ISIS, the kingdom cracked down even further on official foreign aid: Saudi charities can't send money abroad and cannot operate abroad except through the King Salman Humanitarian Aid and Relief Centre or the Saudi Red Crescent, per the Saudi embassy in London, which set out this state of affairs in a churlish response to a media investigation into Saudi money and ISIS. Saudi authorities even banned the collection of cash contributions in mosques and public places, which was once a motherlode for the Afghan jihad.

Dawa Today

Saudi Arabia's dawa apparatus seemed to have stretched beyond its limits in the 1990s, but it is still constantly evolving, to this day. One of its newest theaters is China. Spurred by the thousands of Chinese workers who have come to Saudi Arabia in the last decade—even the new train from Mecca to Medina was financed by China—many of whom converted to Islam, as well as a "China fever" among Saudi missionary preachers, the phenomenon shows how Saudi missionary impulses can adapt to new economic realities. In fact, it was developed particularly quickly and ad hoc because Saudi Arabians were annoyed that thousands of foreign, non-Muslim workers were working in their two holiest cities, as Mohammed Turki Al-Sudairi has argued in his seminal research on China dawa. Enlisting the help of Chinese students at the Islamic University of Medina, Dawa Ministry staff worked to convert thousands of Chinese workers, often in large groups. One video from 2012 shows 245 new Chinese converts joyfully embracing each other in a public square and posing for photos with a Saudi sheikh.

This ongoing internal dawa within Saudi Arabia is significant in itself, because it stands to affect the pool of over eleven million migrant workers who now live there. Sometimes this backfires, as noted in Indonesia, but even if a small fraction of them convert, it yields a sizeable population of new, Saudi-influenced Muslims. Thousands of Filipino migrant workers, for example, have converted to Islam in the kingdom. In 1988, the Dawa Ministry set up a Co-Operative Office for

Dawa and Guidance in Riyadh, which claims to have converted over 15,000 migrant workers as of 2009. One of its leaders was a Filipino preacher and convert to Islam named Sheikh Abdul Qadir al-Alabani.

Dawa inside the kingdom is also cost-effective. Perhaps in reflection of this, the Dawa Ministry's foreign expenditures have been steadily decreasing in material terms from 2013 to 2017. The Ministry logged a decrease in most categories of its activities, from 382,000 missionary speeches to 347,000 and from 70,211 seminars to 16,644. However, less labor-intensive modes of dawa, like Arabic Qurans distributed overseas, have increased, from about 94,000 to 203,000.

The kingdom in general is much less flush than it was in the golden age of dawa. The price of oil plummeted in 2014 and its revenues never fully recovered. The kingdom is basically a rentier state and owes a lot to its citizens (who pay no taxes), including free healthcare, energy subsidies, and jobs, and has been in a bind while figuring out how to maintain their expected quality of life as oil prices steadily decrease.

Given the difficulties of diversifying its economy and its challenges at home, plus the costly war in Yemen, Saudi discretionary spending abroad is not what it used to be. MBS is simultaneously trying to create self-reliance in a country where most people are used to huge cash handouts and create new industries outside of oil. Add to this the fact that Saudi Arabia maintains the third-largest military budget in the world, after the US and China, and it is no surprise that the kingdom has been going on the international debt market to sustain spending.

Such material challenges are why it's important not to overstate what Saudi money has or can do and why "Saudi influence"

188   as a catchall explanation for religious fundamentalism in this day and age is unwise.

Turning a Page

Saudi Arabia usually hovers on the periphery of public discourse, but it periodically experiences events that crater its public image. September 11 was one of them; ISIS was another, to the extent that it became known that ISIS styled itself as a Wahhabi state; the cold-blooded murder of the journalist Jamal Khashoggi in 2018 was still another.

In the US, one of the most surprising developments is that the US–Saudi relationship is now a partisan issue. "In my decades in Washington, I've never seen anything like it," said Riedel. Both Democrats and Republicans have made pointed statements, particularly in relation to the ongoing war in Yemen, about slowing arms sales. In 2017, arguing against President Trump's first big arms deal to Saudi Arabia, Senator Bernie Sanders cited "Saudi Arabia's export of religion to Indonesia" on the Senate floor. The chilling murder of Khashoggi in late 2018, which caused a much larger firestorm than the kingdom likely anticipated, aggravated this state of affairs. In June 2019, Democratic senator Chris Murphy, put forth a bipartisan resolution with the Republican senator Todd Young of Indiana to force a vote on the US–Saudi relationship.

For all his media blitzes, MBS does not have a considered leadership style and he tends to accompany every ambitious new initiative with a few huge blunders. Despite recent overtures toward tourism and entertainment, no Saudi royals will discuss the human rights abuses that are increasingly dominating the image of the kingdom broad: its free dispensation of

the death penalty, show trials, detention, torture, harassment,
solitary confinement, the "unacceptably broad definition of terrorism" it uses to crack down on its own civilians.

But Saudi Arabia remains America's number one weapons client and President Donald Trump seemed to affirm the title invented by King Fahd in 1970 when he greeted the kingdom, the site of his very first state visit abroad in 2017, as the "the nation that serves as custodian of the two holiest sites in the Islamic Faith."

In the summer of 2018, I briefed several members of the US National Security Council, upon request, about Gulf proselytization abroad. They were wracking their brains about the effects of Saudi and Gulf dawa in the Muslim world. There was, noted one member, "a lot of congressional angst toward Saudi Arabia." In terms of places that had been significantly affected by Saudi proselytization, they were "loathe to touch Pakistan," but were seeking "quick wins," presumably on the ideological front, elsewhere: the Balkans, Southeast Asia, the Sahel. Beating back conservative Salafism, to them, would be a step toward fighting terrorism.

"But what we're struggling with on an intellectual level," admitted one woman present, "is asking the Saudis to stop proselytization on one hand and then rebuild Yemen and put millions of dollars towards counterextremism programs and intelligence on the other. . . . So we want them to stop, but also keep going."

To their credit, most of them, including members of the State Department and the CIA, were aware of the diffuse nature of the Saudi Dawa Ministry and the multifarious nature of Saudi charity in general. We had come a long way from the 9/11

190   Commission, whose 2004 report already feels like a cultural artifact. Its authors wrote: "What should Americans expect from their government in the struggle against Islamist terrorism? The goals seem unlimited: Defeat terrorism anywhere in the world." This is not a helpful goalpost, to say the least.

But even the idea of quick "ideological wins" against "Salafism" or "Wahhabism" is unrealistic. If there is anything that the three cases examined in this book have shown, it's that Salafism is simply a part of most of their religious landscapes now, due in significant part to the twentieth-century Saudi campaign, but no longer exclusively sustained by the kingdom, or by any Gulf country's investments.

Can America, and the West, learn to live with a world where "fundamentalist" or conservative Islam is a permanent part of the religious spectrum? It must. But it can also take heart that two decades of pressure on Saudi Arabia have not been fruitless: Saudi dawa is largely aboveground today and it's unlikely that the outrageous, black-box terror financing of Al Qaeda in the 1990s will be repeated.

And Saudi Arabia's foreign engagements today are focused closer to home: Yemen, Lebanon, Syria, often clashing directly with Iran or other Gulf states. While the tremendous proselytization energy of the twentieth century is unlikely to reach the same heights, the apparatus set up by the kingdom chugs on in much of the Muslim world.

A Multipolar Islamic World

Saudi Arabia pioneered a novel, global proselytization program in the twentieth century and its success has spurred many imitators. Each has their unique own call to dawa. Why settle for

Saudi money when you could also have Qatari money, Emirati money, and/or Kuwaiti money? (This is exactly what happened in Kosovo.) Around the world today, Qatar, which has an intense regional rivalry with Saudi Arabia, patronizes the Muslim Brotherhood—style Islamists that Saudi Arabia despises, and the UAE often funds projects with a Sufi and interfaith bent. It's true that neither of them are custodians of the two holiest places in Islam, but, in many of their charity recipients' minds, they're close enough.

The Salafi charity model of proselytization plus aid, which was perfected by Saudi Arabia in Palestine, Afghanistan, and the Balkans, is also now commonplace. When Salafi charities from Kuwait go to Syria today, they always bring Salafi books and leaflets alongside food and medicine.

Iran, whose revolution deeply impressed Muslims in the countries visited in this book, is no longer a major player outside the Middle East. Its main commitments today are in its backyard: Iraq, the Syrian civil war, the Yemeni civil war, Lebanon. But Iran-funded Islamic centers outside the Middle East tend to foreground cultural diplomacy and not major religious dawa. The Iranian center in Jakarta, for instance, is more of a gathering place for the city's Afghan and Pakistani refugees than a serious node of foreign influence, and the Iranian cultural center in downtown Sarajevo holds calligraphy classes and stocks travel brochures about tourism in Iran.

"It's not between Iran and Saudi Arabia," said MBS, in 2018. "It's between Iran and Saudi Arabia and UAE and Egypt and Kuwait and Bahrain and Yemen, a lot of countries around the world. So what we want to be sure of is that, whatever they want to do, they do it within their borders."

As seen in Kosovo and the greater Balkans, Turkey is the major new global Islamic power to watch in the next decade, with its bid for cultural and economic influence along the territories of the former Ottoman Empire, but also even in places where it has no major historical connection. In the last fifteen years, Turkey's trade with African countries has grown six-fold to $17.5 billion. There are now over forty Turkish embassies in Africa. Turkey's largest overseas military base is in Mogadishu, Somalia, where there is also a Recep Tayyip Erdoğan Hospital. There is a direct flight from Istanbul to Kano. Throughout the Balkans and now in Africa, Turkey positions itself as a more liberal Sunni alternative to Saudi Salafism and Iranian Shiism. Turkey is a new player in terms of modern global dawa, but from another angle, it's a return to form: it was the Ottomans, after all, who were the custodians of the two holy mosques in Mecca and Medina for more than four hundred years.

For much of the Muslim world, the twentieth century was the Saudi century. Today, the Islamic world, much like the post−Cold War world in general, is a multipolar one. Even if the kingdom reverses its current intentions to diversify its economy and shifts gears once more toward dawa, its international brand has acquired a lot of baggage. Saudi money everywhere carries the whiff of "Saudi money."

The last two decades of international scrutiny of Saudi Arabia may even have been productive, because the charitable components of its foreign aid is not negligible. In Nigeria, Indonesia, and Kosovo, local Islamic authorities have been reanimating Saudi infrastructure with their own traditions. This was put well by Nur Djuli, a onetime member of the Free

Aceh guerrilla movement whom I met in Indonesia's westernmost province, which has resisted Saudi proselytization while
accepting Saudi charity.

"We can keep their money," he said. "But we don't need their
ideas." That might just be the future of Saudi money in the world.

This book would not have been possible without the support of a large number of people. Thanks to Jimmy So and Nick Lemann at Columbia Global Reports for believing in this book ever since the pitch. Many thanks also to CGR's Camille McDuffie and Miranda Sita. I'm grateful to the Pulitzer Center on Crisis Reporting for funding my initial research into Salafism in Southeast Asia and the Balkans. I'm indebted to Phil Fisher and Jill Abramson at Harvard; Andreas Harsono, Ahsan Ridhoi, Noorhaidi Hasan, Ulil Abshar-Abdalla, and Rio Tuasikal in Indonesia; Aminu Abubakar, Mustapha Muhammad, Kabiru Haruna Isa, and Sani Yakubu Adam in Nigeria; and Kastriot Jahaj, Xhabir Hamiti, and Visar Duriqi in Kosovo. Thanks to David Weinberg for helping me interpret Dawa Ministry documents. The Fulbright Commission generously supported my research into Saudi dawa for a year, and I'm grateful for the input of Adam Hanieh, Sian Hawthorne, Nima Mina, and Husam al-Mallak at the School of Oriental and African Studies. Thanks to Toby Mathiessen who provided thoughtful feedback on this manuscript. And thanks to my parents and sister for their peerless support.

Madawi al-Rasheed, *A History of Saudi Arabia*. The best single-volume nonfiction book about the making of modern Saudi Arabia from one of its preeminent academics, who now lives in exile in London. Her body of work gives the best sense of the fragility and built-in chaos of the Saudi state, the dissenting tendencies of its youth, and the malleability of its central power-sharing agreement.

Abdul Rahman Munif, *Cities of Salt*. This 1984 novel, the first of a quintet, is a seminal entry in the subgenre Amitav Ghosh dubbed "Petrofiction" and brings to life better than any documentary the sea change that came to Saudi Arabia with the discovery of oil. It depicts Saudi society from Bedouins to villagers to royals with operatic sweep, imagining the humorous mutual unintelligibility of their early encounters with overeager Americans and the grim realities of their corporate dreams. Munif was obsessed with the idea that oil was a gift to and a "chance" for the Gulf to build a better society, but his criticism of how those resources were managed was so provocative that his Saudi citizenship was eventually stripped from him.

Vijay Prashad, *The Darker Nations: A People's History of the Third World*. The Marxist scholar's alternative history of the Cold War first drew my attention for its unique take on the emergence of Saudi dawa vis-à-vis the postcolonial Non-Aligned Movement. In his view, Saudi Arabia's canniest move was allying with the United States in the face of defiant new liberation ideologies, and it paid off. The rest of the book, about the rise and disillusionment of postcolonial nation projects (the now-defunct Third World), the wide-ranging effects of the IMF policies, and the emergence of the neoliberal consensus, is equally thought-provoking.

Wilfred Thesiger, *Arabian Sands*. One of the greatest travel books of all time, like a hard, polished diamond. Thesiger's epic journeys across the arid Empty Quarter of what is now Saudi Arabia, embedded with Bedouin tribes, have the feeling of the far past, although they took place less than a century ago and some of his companions are still alive. The violently anti-modern Thesiger already resented the encroachments of Ibn Saud on the desert way of life. I read his book feverishly in my youth, and again on the plane to and from Saudi Arabia as an adult. When I finally visited the quiet Saudi desert, I could not but see it through his eyes, and almost tasted the camel-liver-flavored water he drank without complaint on his peregrinations.

198   Maria Todorova, *Imagining the Balkans*. An erudite, belletrist critical work that reframed how I think about this diverse region that many people still only know through its recent wars. Todorova unpacks the construction of the Balkans as both a counterpart to and uneasy part of "Europe" and shows how its Ottoman legacy is much deeper than one of architecture, because its millet system explains how the multiethnic states came to be. It's impossible to forget her account of "Balkanism" and all its related tropes, which roared back to life when Yugoslavia dissolved.

Tom Boellstorff, *The Gay Archipelago*. Why is this academic book about the lives of queer Indonesians still my single favorite book about the country that has been like a second home to me? I wish I could tell you more precisely, but I tend to press it upon strangers and new arrivals and let them figure it out for themselves. Not a week goes by when I don't reference his ideas about dubbing culture, Bahasa Indonesia (the national language), and mass media. To me, one of the reasons Saudi dawa and Salafi ideas proved so influential in modern Indonesia is the rapid dissemination of ideas in the world's fourth-largest country, from the perceived "deviance" of Shia to the "blasphemy" of a politician. And Boellstorff's brilliant but accessible account of the unique Indonesian nation-state is the best way to wrap your head around the idea of a country of 15,000+ islands.

Glenna Gordon and Carmen McCain, *Diagram of the Heart*. Researching *The Call* prompted my very first trips to West Africa, and though my own subject matter was rather grim, I fell in love with Kano, a vibrant center of Sahel culture. In looking to learn more about other sides of northern Nigeria, I found this delightful photo book about the cottage industry of Muslim romance novels written by women. The intimate images show a world not untouched by religious fundamentalism—some of the women have been censored by the Hisbah and others sell their books in markets that have been attacked by Boko Haram—but, at the same time, on discrete affective and imaginative planes. It's a portal into this unique region and the lives of its women who dare to create.

Millard Burr and Robert O. Collins, *Alms for Jihad: Charity and Terrorism in the Islamic World*. This highly researched volume on Islamic charities, with a chapter dedicated to ones from Saudi Arabia, was forced off shelves almost as soon as it was published. The Saudi billionaire named Khalid bin Mahfouz, who was named in its pages as an alleged financier of Al Qaeda, sued the authors for libel under the UK's notoriously broad laws. Mahfouz died in 2009 and the book's full text is now available on the Internet Archive, but it's worth tracking down a copy if you can find it in a library or reading room near you.

NOTES

INTRODUCTION

14 The 411 rally was billed as an aksi damai: In the 1980s, in an eerie historical parallel, the now-defunct Darul Islam fundamentalist group tried to organize a show of Islamic solidarity in Jakarta, but it fell apart. See Solahudin, *The Roots of Terrorism in Indonesia: From Darul Islam to Jem'ah Islamiyah*, tr. Dave McRae (Ithaca, NY: Cornell University Press, 2013), 108.

15 This was a turning point for political Islam in Indonesia: In the Suharto years, for instance, the Foreign Minister, Mochtar Kusumaatmadja, said that "Indonesia was not a Muslim country" and the Suharto administration professed to "not admit a special public place for Islam." See Michael Leifer, "The Islamic Factor in Indonesia's Foreign Policy: A Case of Functional Ambiguity," *Islam in Foreign Policy* (Cambridge: Cambridge University Press, 1983), 154.

15 quickly consolidated his stature as a populist religious vigilante: Greg Fealy, "Islamic Radicalism in Indonesia: The Faltering Revival?" *Southeast Asian Affairs* (2004), 114.

CHAPTER ONE

23–24 when the wireless telegraph was introduced in

Riyadh in the 1920s: David [199]
Commins, *The Wahhabi Mission and Saudi Arabia* (London: I. B. Tauris, 2006), 97-98.

25 From the start, Wahhabism was tied to persecution, expansion, and conquest: Hamad Redissi, "The Refutation of Wahhabism in Arabic Sources, 1745–1932," in *Kingdom Without Borders*, ed. Madawi Al-Rasheed (Oxford: Oxford University Press, 2008), 164.

25 Abd al-Wahhab and his troops waged dozens of battles in and around the region: Redissi, 164.

26 forbidding such behaviors as celebrating the new millennium: Sadakat Kadri, *Heaven on Earth: A Journey Through Shari'a Law.* London: Vintage (2013), 200.

27 Wahhabism and Salafism found some "elective affinities" in the twentieth century: Redissi, 177.

30 foreigners helped consolidate the Wahhabi mission: Commins, 99.

30 helped preach Wahhabism to unconverted Bedouin tribes in the desert: Chanfi Ahmed, *West African 'ulamā' and Salafism in Mecca and Medina: jawab al-Ifrīqī— the response of the African.* Leiden/Boston: Brill, (2015), 6.

30 He did reopen the hajj to non-Wahhabis in 1925: The number of hajj pilgrims per year has increased

200   from 90,000 in 1926 to about 2 million in 1979 to about 2.35 million today according to Gilles Kepel, *Jihad: The Trail of Political Islam* (Cambridge, MA: Belknap, 2002), 75. This does not include *umrah* trips to visit Mecca and Medina outside the annual five-day pilgrimage festival. The crush of pilgrims has sometimes resulted in catastrophes like a 2015 stampede where 2,000 people died.

30   **almost bankrupted the kingdom:** Millard Burr and Robert O. Collins, *Alms for Jihad: Charity and Terrorism in the Islamic World.* (Cambridge: Cambridge University Press, 2006), 106.

31   **Until 1951, there were only three ministries in its whole government:** Madawi al-Rasheed, *A History of Saudi Arabia* (Cambridge: Cambridge University Press, 2010), 86.

31   **Wahhabi clerics were allowed to steer ministries:** Gold, 77.

31   **They also controlled the directorate of "religious research, Islamic legal rulings, Islamic propagation, and guidance":** Gold, 78.

31–32   **It was not even well formed at the time it was exported:** Madawi Al-Rasheed, *Contesting the Saudi State: Islamic Voices from a New Generation.* Cambridge: Cambridge University Press (2007), 103–104.

32   **there were hardly any scholars of note from there in the early twentieth century:** Al-Rasheed, 103.

32   **peaking at $113.3 billion a year in 1981:** René Rieger, *Saudi Arabian Foreign Relations: Diplomacy and Mediation in Conflict Resolution,* London: Routledge (2016), 37–38.

32   **internal laws against mixed-gender socializing, singing the Quran melodically, and depicting women on TV:** Burr and Collins, 105.

33   **Some went as "jihad tourists":** Sageman, Marc, *Understanding Terror Networks,* University of Pennsylvania Press, 2004, 57–58.

33   **He tripled the budget of the Committee to Prevent Vice and Promote Virtue:** Hammond, 156.

33   **"Islamized" the curricula of all the Saudi universities:** Robert Lacey, *Inside the Kingdom* (London: Arrow, 2009), 50.

34   **the influential institution of the "religious attaché":** Lacey, 95.

35   **"No limit should be put on expenditures for the propagation of Islam":** Lacey, 95.

35   **Saudi revenues flow directly to the royal family and are not reported to anyone:** House 2012: 25.

35   **The Dawa Ministry has a staff of over 9,500 people in the kingdom:** Kingdom of Saudi Arabia, Ministry of Islamic Affairs, da'wah, and Guidance, "Statistical Yearbook for the Fiscal Year 1438/1439" [Arabic], 2017, Available online at: https://www.moia.gov.sa/Statistics/Pages/Details.aspx?ID=9.

36   **its activities included sponsoring 22,146 conversions to Islam:** ibid

36   **the official Saudi Red Crescent budget for 2002 was about $10 million:** Burr and Collins, 31.

36   **work through hundreds of local affiliates:** Kepel, 73.

37   **The most important international Saudi charity, the Muslim World League:** Commins, 112.

37   **In 1974, its stated annual budget was $50 million:** Gold, 99.

37   **under the leadership of the stringent Wahhabi ideologue Abd al-Aziz ibn-Baz:** Gold, 119.

37   **It also dispatched nearly a thousand missionaries:** Gold, 121.

37   **the Saudi government had given it over $1.33 billion since its founding:** Burr and Collins, 34.

38   **to explain the League's goals and its potential as a "bulwark against Communism":** Deepa Kumar, "The Right Kind of 'Islam,'" *Journalism Studies*, 19:8 (2018), 1088.

38   **the discourse inside MWL circles was fairly erudite:** Ziauddin Sardar, *An Early Crescent: the Future of Knowledge and the Environment in Islam* (Mecca: Muslim World League, October 1987), 16.

38   **somewhat more hardline than the MWL:** Gold, 79.

38   **its fundraising target, under Prince Salman's oversight, was $266.6 million:** Burr and Collins, 36.

38–39   **it has been active in many of the high-profile conflicts involving Muslim communities in the last three decades:** Burr and Collins, 31.

39   **at least 1,500 mosques:** Benjamin, *Kingdom of the Unjust*, 103.

39   **at least $10 million to build mosques in the US:** Gold, 112.

39   **volume of Islamic rulings of Bin Baz:** "Shaykh `Abdul-`Azeez Bin Baz," FatwaIslam.com, 2019. Available at http://www.fatwaislam.com/fis/index.cfm?scn=search_sch&sch=1.

39   **photocopying is theoretically forbidden by Salafi doctrine:** Laurent Bonnefoy, *Salafism in Yemen: Transnationalism and Religious Identity* (Oxford: Oxford University Press, 2012), 141.

202   40   **in 2002 there were 264, by one count, with combined assets of $550 million:** Burr and Collins, 38.

40   **the Saudi government subsidized about 80 percent of these charities' expenditures:** Burr and Collins, 38.

40   **printed 15 million copies of Islamic books:** Burr and Collins, 38.

40   **no subsidiary could receive funds without the personal approval of the foundation's director:** Secretary of State, "Terrorist Financing—Updated Nonpaper on Al Haramayn," Wikileaks Cable: 03STATE23994_a, dated January 28, 2003. Available at: https://wikileaks.org/plusd /cables/03STATE23994_a.html.

41   **The mysterious Islamic Benevolence Committee was founded in 1987:** Burr and Collins, 45.

41   **smaller charities utilize a paperless system of finance called** *hawala:* Jean-Charles Brisard, "Terrorism Financing: Roots and Trends of Saudi Terrorism Financing," Report prepared for the President of the Security Council United Nations (December 19, 2002), 8.

41   **eliciting solidarity for besieged Muslim communities:** On this, see *Reasserting International Islam: A Focus on the Organization of the Islamic Conference and Other Islamic Institutions* by Saad S. Khan (Oxford: Oxford University Press, 2001).

41   **"An avuncular [Gamel Abdul] Nasser shepherded around a cagey Faisal":** Vijay Prashad, *The Darker Nations: A People's History of the Third World* (New York: The New Press 2007), 263.

42   **as opposed to through organic, historic, or cultural ties:** "The United States is the most dangerous thing to us," King Fahd told a young Prince Bandar al Sultan, who would grow up to become the Saudi ambassador to the U.S. "We have no cultural connection with them…no ethnic connection to them… no religious connection…no language connection…no political connection." (Patrick Tyler, *A World of Trouble: The White House and the Middle East—from the Cold War to the War on Terror.*)

42   **the current received wisdom that Saudi fundamentalism has been deleterious for the Muslim world:** Gold, 8.

42   **Saudi influence could steer it back on course:** Kumar, "The Right Kind of 'Islam,'" 1084.

43   **$6 billion in foreign aid:** Rachel Bronson, *Thicker Than Oil: America's Uneasy Partnership with Saudi Arabia* (Oxford: Oxford University Press, 2006), 129.

43   "a helpful Saudi footprint placed so unobtrusively that one gust of wind could erase its traces": Bronson, 131.

43   **Safari Club:** Toby Matthiesen, "Saudi Arabia and the Cold War" in *Salman's Legacy: The Dilemmas of a New Era in Saudi Arabia,* ed. Madawi al-Rasheed (London: Hurst & Co., 2018), 230–233.

43   **Washington saw the kingdom's lack of financial transparency as an advantage:** Roger Hardy, "Ambivalent Ally: Saudi Arabia and the "War on Terror," in *Kingdom Without Borders*, ed. Madawi Al-Rasheed (Oxford: Oxford University Press, 2008), 104.

44   **provided training and technology to the kingdom in the 1970s:** Robert Dreyfuss, *Devil's Game: How the United States Helped Unleash Fundamentalist Islam* (New York: Metropolitan Books, 2006), 168–171.

44   **Saudi Arabia's government spent an estimated $3 billion:** Hardy, 101–102.

44   **"Jihad and the rifle alone: no negotiations, no conferences, and no dialogues":** Burr and Collins, 32.

44   **"Prince Salman Abdel Aziz had a budget of $27 million per year":** Burr and Collins, 32.

44   **Saudi Arabia bet on religion and political quietism:** Kepel, 62.

45   **"the stage of jihad in the battalions of the dawa to your Lord":** Michael Farquhar, *Circuits of Faith: Migration, Education, and the Wahhabi Mission* (Palo Alto: Stanford University Press, 2016), 113–114.

45   **scholarship students from Nigeria, Indonesia, Yugoslavia, Palestine, Jordan, and South Vietnam:** Omari H. Kokole, "African-Arab Relations: A Cultural Perspective," in *India Quarterly*, vol. 40, no. 1 (1984), 36.

46   **Over 60 percent of the university's inaugural staff were foreign:** Farquhar, 94.

46   **a refuge for members of the Muslim Brotherhood:** Farquhar, 96.

46   **Bin Baz, who served as its second president:** Commins, 112.

46   **asserted that the earth, and not the sun, was at the center of the universe:** "Is the earth revolving? Sheikh Saleh Al-Fawzan," [Arabic] 2015. Available at: https://www.youtube .com/watch?v=r7sO9vBecms &feature=youtu.be.

46   **Umm Al-Qura University in Mecca and Imam Muhammad ibn Saud university in Riyadh:** Zaman, 153.

46   **competed with the likes of Al-Azhar:** Al-Azhar also started fragmenting after it was nationalized by Egypt in 1961. See

204   Masooda Bano, "At the Tipping Point? Al-Azhar's Growing Crisis of Moral Authority," *International Journal of Middle East Studies*, vol. 50, no. 4 (2018), 715–734.

47   **Freedom House began to publish reports about "Wahhabi ideology":** Ismail, 118.

47   ***The Guardian* went with "Salafee":** Hammond, 147.

47   **Saddam Hussein attacked the kingdom as an "American protectorate" for allowing US troops on its holy land:** Kepel, 206.

47   **requiring all donations collected by charities to be deposited in a fund administered by a Saudi prince:** Burr and Collins, 39–40.

47   **"the Kingdom of Saudi Arabia is a state that supports terrorism":** Gold, 193.

48   **"when confronted by legal challenges, the United States and the United Nations were often forced to unfreeze assets":** The 9/11 Commission Report: final report of the National Commission on Terrorist Attacks upon the United States. Washington, D.C.: National Commission on Terrorist Attacks upon the United States (2004), 381. Accessible at: http:// govinfo.library.unt.edu/911 /report/911Report.pdf.

48   **"They point a very strong finger at Saudi Arabia being the principle financier":** Eleanor Clift, "The Missing Pages of the 9/11 Report," *The Daily Beast*, January 12, 2015. Accessible at: https://www .thedailybeast.com/the-missing -pages-of-the-911-report.

48   **"the kernel of evil, the prime mover, the most dangerous opponent":** Kumar, 1081.

48   **"In the past we may have been naive in our giving":** Burr and Collins, 30.

48   **"You go to Friday prayers. You could stand there and say, 'Please help.'":** Brisard, "Terrorism Financing," 5.

49   **introduced banking regulations that temporarily stopped all private charities from sending funds abroad:** Salwa Ismail, "Producing "Reformed Islam:" A Saudi Contribution to the U.S. Projects of Global Governance" in *Kingdom Without Borders*, ed. Madawi Al-Rasheed. (Oxford: Oxford University Press, 2008), 122.

49   **In 2003, the kingdom briefly considered recalling its religious attachés:** Council on Foreign Relations, "Terrorist Financing: Report of an Independent Task Force, Sponsored by the Council on Foreign Relations." New York: CFR (2002), 22. Accessible at:

http://www.cfr.org/pdf
/Terrorist_Financing_TF.pdf.

49   Saudis who wanted to donate
to WAMY could not merely
transfer money to well-publicized
bank accounts but had to do it in
person and get a receipt: Caryle
Murphy, "9/11 Forces Change to
Saudi's Global Religious Mission,"
GlobalPost (September 6, 2011).
Available at https://www.pri.org
/stories 2011-09-06/911-forces
-change-saudis-global-religious
-mission.

50   the American fixation
with Saudi textbooks began:
Ismail, 123.

50   Problematic passages
included those addressing Jews,
Christians, "infidels," minority
Muslim sects: The Anti-
Defamation League, "Teaching Hate
and Violence: Problematic Passages
from Saudi State Textbooks for the
2018–19 School Year" (2018), 9.
Available at https://www.adl.org
/media/12180/download.

51   "obey their current rulers
at home while at the same time
fostering the spirit of jihad
abroad": Madawi al-Rasheed,
"The Minaret and the Palace:
Obedience at Home and Rebellion
Abroad," in *Kingdom Without
Borders,* ed. Madawi Al-Rasheed
(Oxford: Oxford University Press,
2008), 201.

52   ISIS, claims to be the   205
world's true Wahhabi state:
Cole Bunzel, "The Kingdom and
the Caliphate: Duel of the Islamic
States." Carnegie Endowment
for International Peace (February
18, 2016). Available at: https://
carnegieendowment.org/2016
/02/18/kingdom-and-caliphate
-duel-of-islamic-states-pub
-62810.

52   set up its own printing
press in Mosul in 2014: Shiraz
Maher, *Salafi-Jihadism: The
History of an Idea* (London: Hurst,
2016), 211.

52   destroying ancient holy
sites from Palmyra to Timbuktu
follows a distinctly Wahhabi
logic: Ahmed, 537.

52   Saudi-affiliated
fundamentalists destroyed
more than thirty Sufi shrines
in the early 2000s: "Wahabism
[sic] in Ethiopia as 'Cultural
Imperialism.'" Wikileaks Cable:
09ADDISABABA1674_a, dated
July 15, 2009. Available at: https://
wikileaks.org/plusd/cables/09
ADDISABABA1674_a.html.

52   As one Saudi intelligence
official observed in 2005: Thomas
Hegghammer, *Jihad in Saudi Arabia:
Violence and Pan-Islamism Since
1979.* (Cambridge: Cambridge
University Press, 2012), 238.

206 CHAPTER TWO

53 probably the first accounts of Westerners wringing hands over the "Arabization" of "innocent" and "peaceful" Indonesian Islam: Bonnefoy, 9.

54 they were actually punished for showing an interest in Wahhabism: Ahmed, 161.

56 he went into exile deep in the Sumatran jungle: Audrey Kahin, *Islam, Nationalism and Democracy: A Political Biography of Mohammad Natsir*. Singapore: NUS Press (2012), 131.

57 From the start, DDII was closely affiliated with the Muslim World League in Mecca: Noorhaidi Hasan, *Laskar Jihad: Islam, Militancy, and the Quest for Identity in Post-New Order Indonesia* (Ithaca: Cornell University Press, 2006), 40.

57 the latter did not bother to open a separate office in Indonesia: Martin Van Bruinessen, "Indonesian Muslims and Their Place in the Larger World of Islam" in: *Indonesia Rising: The Repositioning of Asia's Third Giant*, ed. Anthony Reid. Singapore: ISEAS–Yusof Ishak Institute (2011), 121.

57 Natsir's personal diplomacy won him an open-ended *tazkiya*: Keppel, 63.

57 DDII became a vessel for other Saudi dawa bodies: Hasan, 41.

57 half of the Supreme World Council of Mosques' $29 million budget was designated for Southeast Asia: James Piscatori, "Islamic Values and National Interest," in *Islam in Foreign Policy*, ed. Adeed Dawisha (Cambridge: Cambridge University Press, 1983), 46.

58 He was most paranoid about Christian missionary activity in the new Indonesia: Martin van Bruinessen (2002), "Genealogies of Islamic Radicalism in Post-Suharto Indonesia," *South East Asia Research*, 10:2, 117-154, p. 123.

58 It started to print a hugely popular monthly magazine called *Media Dakwah*: Hasan, 41

58 Natsir's work was happening at a true grassroots level: Leifer, 153.

59 were translated into Indonesian and sold briskly, especially in university towns: Martin van Bruinessen, "Ghazwul fikri or Arabisation? Indonesian Muslim responses to globalisation," in: *Dynamics of Southeast Asian Muslims in the Era of Globalization*, ed. Ken Miichi and Omar Farouk. Tokyo: International Cooperation Agency Research Institute (JICA-RI) (2013), 23.

60 "I read his book from cover to cover when I was in high school in Central Java": Interestingly the person who translated Ali

Shari'ati's book into Bahasa Indonesia, Amin Rais, would later become a conservative MP and a strident anti-Shi'a voice.

60 **who would become one of Indonesia's most prominent jihadists:** Solahudin, 6.

60 **nevertheless DDII became a primary agent of the campaign against them:** Martin van Bruinessen, "Global and Local in Indonesian Islam," *Southeast Asian Studies* (Kyoto) vol. 37, no. 2 (1999), 52.

60 **Its publications shifted from Muslim Brotherhood texts to anti-Shia screeds:** Bruinessen, "Ghazwul fikri or Arabisation?" 14.

62 **attended the inaugural conference of the World Assembly of Muslim Youth in 1972 in Riyadh:** WAMY also held its eleventh conference in 2010 in Jakarta.

63 **"Once you accept that, you're on their payroll for life":** I previously wrote about this in a 2017 article on Saudi scholarships in Indonesia: "Saudi Arabia Quietly Spreads its Brand of Puritanical Islam in Indonesia," Voice of America, January 17, 2017. Accessible at: https://www.voanews.com/east-asia-pacific/saudi-arabia-quietly-spreads-its-brand-puritanical-islam-indonesia.

64 **LIPIA's predecessor, the LPBA language institute, was set** up by the Saudi ambassador at the time: Hasan, 48.

66 **As of 2018, 2,230 Indonesians had graduated IUM since its founding:** www.enwbe.iu.edu.sa.

66 **in 2004, 3,528 Indonesian students were in Egypt, mostly at Al-Azhar:** Fealy and Bubalo, 51.

66 **sought alternative course of study at Al-Madinah International University, or MEDIU:** Chaplin 225.

66 **that offers online degree programs for any interested undergraduates and postgraduates, in both Arabic and English:** Chris Chaplin, "Salafism in Indonesia: Translocal Islamic Activism amongst Urban Muslims in Yogyakarta" [manuscript draft] (2019), 225.

69 **Soccer players on their first trips abroad watched their drinking buddies burn alive:** Michael Paterniti, "The Heartbreak Boys of Coogee Beach," *GQ* (October 11, 2004).

71 **The Bali bombing project was plotted in various forms starting in 1985:** Solahudin, 123.

72 **JI set up more than twenty Salafi-jihadi schools across Indonesia and Malaysia:** Solahudin, 161.

72 **Nasir Abbas branched off to the Philippines:** The Southern

208   Philippines would become a hotbed of terrorism. While Abbas was there, Osama bin Laden's brother-in-law Muhammad Jamal Khalifa headed the Saudi charity IIRO, a branch of the Muslim World League (Gold, 153). The office was later revealed to be a "legal front to conceal the transfer of al-Qaeda funding and materiel to the [militant] Abu Sayyaf Group" (Wikileaks Cable 05MANILA2356_a).

73   **Laskar Jihad's activities were supported by the humanitarian branch of DDII:** "Defenders of the Faithful: Dewan Dakwah Islamiyah Indonesia (DDII)," Wikileaks Cable: 07JAKARTA 660_a, dated March 8, 2007. Available at: https://wikileaks.org /plusd/cables/07JAKARTA660_a .html.

74   **As recently as 2015, the Saudi ambassador and former religious attaché actively attended events at ICBB:** "Building opening of Ma'had Tahfizh Abu Bakar As-Sidiq," Islamic Center Bin Baz (May 17, 2015). Available at: http://www.binbaz.or.id/berita/37 -kabar-berita/435-peresmian -gedung-mahad-tahfizh-abu -bakar-as-sidiq-icbb.

74   **residents refused to allow the ICBB school to expand its campus:** "Expansion of Bin Baz Islamic Center Denied by Piyungan Residents," Islam Indonesia, (September 29, 2015). Available at:

http://www.fiqhislam.com/agenda /islam-indonesia/1429-perluasan -islamic-center-bin-baz-ditolak -warga-piyungan.

74   **at least four suicide bombings from this decade in Indonesia ended up killing only the bomber:** Stephen Wright, "IS Recruits in SE Asia a Rising Threat Despite Weak Attacks," *The Jakarta Post* (July 14, 2016). https://www.thejakartapost.com /seasia/2016/07/14/is-recruits-in -se-asia-a-rising-threat-despite -weak-attacks.html; "Failed Suicide Bombing at Central Java Police Outpost Injures Only Bomber," Coconuts Jakarta (June 4, 2019). https://coconuts.co/jakarta /news/failed-suicide-bombing -at-central-java-police-output -injures-only-bomber/; "Suicide Bomber Attacks Packed Indonesian Church," Fox News (September 25, 2011, last updated November 17, 2014). https://www.foxnews.com /world/suicide-bomber-attacks -packed-indonesian-church; Oliver Holmes, "Man Armed with Suicide Bomb and Axe Attacks Church in Indonesia," *The Guardian* (August 29, 2016). https://www .theguardian.com/world/2016 /aug/29/man-armed-with-suicide -bomb-and-axe-attacks-church -in-indonesia.

75   **The bombings were planned by a deadly new jihadist group called Jamaah Ansharut Daulah:** Kate Lamb, "Families Behind

Indonesia Bombings Belonged to Same Religious Study Group," *The Guardian* (May 15, 2018). Available at https://www.theguardian.com/world/2018/may/15/families-behind-indonesia-bombings-belonged-to-same-religious-study-group-suicide-attacks-east-java.

75 **JAD's spiritual leader is Aman Abdurrahman:** Adi Renaldi, "The Inside Story of JAD, Indonesia's Newest, and Deadliest, Terrorist Group," *Vice Indonesia* (May 31, 2018). Available at https://www.vice.com/en_asia/article/pav339/the-inside-story-of-jad-indonesias-newest-and-deadliest-terrorist-group.

75 **His sermons circulated widely as cassettes:** V. Arianti, "Aman Abdurrahman: Ideologue and 'Commander' of IS Supporters in Indonesia." *Counter Terrorist Trends and Analyses*, vol. 9, no. 2, 2017, 4–9.

75 **He was fluent in Arabic, memorized the Quran, and wrote a book on why Islam and democracy are incompatible:** Rendi Witular, "The Rise of Aman Abdurrahman, IS Master Ideologue," *The Jakarta Post* (January 25, 2016). Available at https://www.thejakartapost.com/news/2016/01/25/the-rise-aman-abdurrahman-is-master-ideologue.html.

75 **Not only did Aman study at LIPIA for seven years:** "Abdurrahman's Profile and Record of Crime," *JPNN* (May 19, 2018). Available at https://www.jpnn.com/news/profil-dan-catatan-tidak-kejahatan-aman-abdurrahman?page=1.

CHAPTER THREE

78 **The Ahmadiyya are a tiny minority in Indonesia:** Saskia Schäfer, "Renegotiating Indonesian Secularism Through Debates on Ahmadiyya and Shi'a," *Philosophy and Social Criticism*, Vol. 41 (4–5) (2015), 498.

78 **In 2011, a mob of 1,500 attacked an Ahmadiyya site in West Java:** M. C. Ricklefs, *Islamisation and Its Opponents in Java: A Political, Social, Cultural and Religious History, c. 1930 to Present* (Singapore: NUS Press, 2012), 321.

78 **threatened "unrest" to the provincial government if they allowed the Ahmadiyya to organize counterprotests there:** A. N. Burhani, "Fundamentalism and Religious Dissent: The LPPI's Mission to Eradicate the Ahmadiyya in Indonesia," *Indonesia and the Malay World*, 44:129 (2016), 150.

79 **Amin Djamaluddin organized the influential national seminar:** Chiara Formichi, "Violence, Sectarianism, and the Politics of Religion: Articulations of Anti-Shi'a Discourses in Indonesia," in *Indonesia* No. 98, (2014), 15.

210 79 **In 2006, a Sunni mob disrupted a Shia celebration of Ashura in East Java:** Institute for Policy Analysis and Conflict "The Anti-Shi'a Campaign in Indonesia" (2016), 19. Available: http://www.understandingconflict.org/en/conflict/read/50/THE-ANTI-Shi'a-MOVEMENT-IN-INDONESIA.

80 **He created a publishing house called Al-Mizan to translate Iranian books:** Al-Mizan means "scales" in Arabic and is also the name of the major Shi'a newspaper in Nigeria, as well as the news website of Iran's judiciary. It is commonly used by Shi'a outfits outside Iran to create a sense of transnational community.

82 **their clothing and lifestyle choices are an expression of their belief that society should be gradually Islamized:** Hasan, *Laskar Jihad*, 31.

82 **The Yogyakarta-based Salafi radio station RadioMuslim gets small donations from its listeners:** Chaplin, 162.

82 **their monthly budget has increased from eight million rupiah in 2011 to thirty-eight million rupiah in 2018:** Chaplin, 162.

82 **classes for women on how to be a good Islamic wife:** "Kelas KPNI." Ar-Rahman Pre-Wedding Academy (Website), AQL Laznas.

Accessible at: https://apwa.wordpress.com/kelas-kpni/. Accessed on 7 April 2019. KPNI stands for "Kursus Pra Nikah Islami," or the "Islamic Pre-Marriage Course."

82 **The Saudi Dawa Ministry's material support of the Indonesian religious attaché has decreased over the last five years:** Kingdom of Saudi Arabia, Ministry of Islamic Affairs, da'wah, and Guidance, "Statistical Yearbook for the Fiscal Year 1438/1439" [Arabic], 2017, Available online at https://www.moia.gov.sa/Statistics/Pages/Details.aspx?ID=9.

83 **the evergreen presidential loser Prabowo:** Bernhard Platzdach, *Islamism in Indonesia: Politics in the Emerging Democracy* (Singapore: ISEAS–Yusof Ishak Institute, 2009), 122.

84 **This admixture of "rejection and admiration":** Bonnefoy, 158.

85 **the image of Saudi Arabia remains strong in both the religious and nonreligious spheres:** Chaplin, Chris (2014). Imagining the Land of the Two Holy Mosques: The social and doctrinal importance of Saudi Arabia in Indonesian Salafi discourse. *ASEAS – Austrian Journal of South-East Asian Studies, 7*(2), 217-236.

86 **The Saudi Charity Campaign promptly set up in the provincial capital of Banda Aceh and donated**

more than $45 million: Krithika Varagur, "Conservative Aceh Shows Limits of Saudi Investment in Indonesia," *Voice of America* (September 13, 2017). Available at https://www.voanews.com/east -asia-pacific/conservative-aceh -shows-limits-saudi-investment -indonesia.

87 **Salafi study groups started popping up at mosques around the province:** Institute for Policy Analysis and Conflict, "The Anti-Salafi Campaign in Aceh" (2016), 19. Available at http://www .understandingconflict.org/en /conflict/read/55/The-Anti-Salafi -Campaign-in-Aceh.

88 **the Free Aceh Movement, which trained in Libya, refused to send members to Saudi Arabia:** Institute for Policy Analysis and Conflict, "The Anti-Salafi Campaign in Aceh" (2016), 16.

89 **"the land that keeps secrets":** "Spreading of Islam in Papua," Report by the Women's Coalition for Papua Reconciliation, Indonesian Christian Church (GKI) of Papua (July 6, 2014). Provided to the author by Dora Balubun.

89 **As of July 2014, the group has circumcised over 7,500 children:** "Spreading of Islam in Papua."

90 **Ustad Fadlan of AFKN Nuu War has also made several appearances at the Saudi Religious Attaché's office:** https:// www.facebook.com/photo.php ?fbid=1289455617755038&set =a.101556673211611&type=3& theater.

CHAPTER FOUR

92 **religious demographics are so contentious that it has not been a question on the census since 1963:** Ousman Kane, "Izala: The Rise of Muslim Reformism in Northern Nigeria," in *Accounting for Fundamentalisms: The Dynamic Character of Movements,* ed. Martin E. Marty and R. Scott Appleby (Chicago: University of Chicago Press, 2004), 491. One estimate from the Pew Center suggests the breakdown is 49 percent Muslim, 48 percent Christian, and the rest of traditional or unspecified faiths. Other estimates flip it and say Nigeria is narrowly a Christian-majority country.

93 **spent so much gold along the way that he deflated gold prices along his route for years:** Omari H. Kokole, "African-Arab Relations: A Cultural Perspective," in *India Quarterly,* vol. 40, no. 1 (1984), 1.

93 **This is not unusual among modern African countries, which were traditionally organized on a horizontal axis:** Hatim M Amiji, "Religion in Afro-Arab Relations: Islam and Culture Change in Modern Africa," UNESCO Symposium on Historical and Socio-cultural Relations between

212   Black Africa and the Arab World, Paris, 1979, 24. Permanent URL: https://unesdoc.unesco.org /ark:/48223/pf0000039400. Accessed July 15, 2019.

94   **About 65 percent of Nigeria Muslims identify as Sufis:** "Chapter 1: Religious Affiliation," Pew Research Center, August 9, 2012, accessed July 12, 2019.

95   **Sufism—which is not a sect like Sunnah and Shia but an approach to Islam:** L. Massington, B. Radtke, W. C. Chittick, F. de Jong, L. Lewisohn, Th. Zarcone, C. Ernst, Françoise Aubin, and J. O. Hunwick, "Taṣawwuf," in: *Encyclopaedia of Islam*, Second Edition, ed. by P. Bearman, Th. Bianquis, C. E. Bosworth, E. van Donzel, W. P. Heinrichs. Consulted online on 29 July 2019. <http://dx.doi .org/10.1163/1573-3912_islam _COM_1188>. First published online: 2012. First print edition: ISBN: 9789004161214, 1960–2007.

95   **so the Saudis were not fighting an uphill battle of ideas there as they were in North Africa:** The key exception is the Horn of Africa, including Somalia, Ethiopia, and Djibouti, where Saudi Arabia was part of a ragtag "Safari Club" founded by a French count to keep Communists out of the region. See Toby Mathiessen, "Saudi Arabia and the Cold War," in Madawi al-Rasheed (ed.), *Salman's Legacy: The Dilemmas of a New Era in Saudi Arabia* (London: Hurst & Co, 2018), 217–233.

95   **The very first international recruitment tour delegation from the International University of Medina:** Ahmed, 146.

95   **There was a Nigerian who went on both of these tours:** Umar Fallata, whose parents had fled British colonial rule in Nigeria, loved Medina so much that he gave lectures on the topic and wrote paeans to the city's charms in local periodicals, like the different kinds of dates one could find there (Ahmed, 117).

95   **both because of its size and its history with the Sokoto Caliphate:** Ahmed, 149

95–96   **In these early tours, IUM delegates downplayed Wahhabism:** Ahmed, 150.

96–97   **to lead a vigorous conversion campaign across Nigeria:** Kane, "Izala: The Rise of Muslim Reformism in Northern Nigeria," 492–493.

97   **Bello loved visiting Saudi Arabia:** John Hunwick, "An African Case Study of Political Islam: Nigeria," *The Annals of the American Academy of Political and Social Science*, Vol. 524, Political Islam (November, 1992), 151.

97   **built schools for, sent cultural envoys to, and offered scholarships:** Kokole, 18.

97   the next military governor gave him even more leverage and free media access: Kane, 493.

97   using open-air sermons, radio, television, and cassette tapes that are still circulated in Kano markets today: Hunwick, 151.

98   Idris worked locally while Gumi traveled back and forth to Mecca: Ramzi Ben Amara, "Shaykh Ismaila Idris (1937–2000): The Founder of the Izala Movement in Nigeria," *Annual Review of Islam in Africa*, 11, 2012, 74-78.

98   Izala attacked various local religious practices like visiting graves: Kane, 499

98   Its preachers even discouraged eating meat slaughtered by Sufis: Kane, 499

98   middle-class Nigerians were the perfect candidates for a movement that encouraged reading texts for yourself: Kane, 494.

98   There were seven hundred nationwide sessions: Muhammad Sani Umar, "Education and Islamic Trends in Northern Nigeria: 1970s–1990s," *Africa Today*, Vol. 48, No. 2 (Summer, 2001), 131.

98   Izala members were very systematic about building physical mosques and schools: Amara, 135.

98–99   Up until 1900, there was only one mosque in all of central Kano: Kabiru Haruna Isa and Muhammad Wada, "The Proliferation of Juma'at Mosques in Kano Metropolis," January 2019.

99   the battle for hearts and minds could be fought elsewhere: Isa and Wada.

99   help at least one businessman who joined the movement: Kane, 498.

99   anyone who recited a Tijaniyya prayer was an "unbeliever" and could be killed: Amara, 139.

100   they threw their support behind Ahmad Sani: Ramzi Ben Amara, "'We Introduced Sharī'a': The Izala Movement in Nigeria as Initiator of Sharī'a-re-implementation in the North of the Country: Some Reflections," in John A. Chesworth and Franz Kogelmann (eds.), *Sharī'a in Africa Today: Reactions and Responses* (Leiden: Brill, 2014), 143.

100   at least one Sufi on the Kano State's sharia implementation committee resigned because of its Salafi domination: Shaykh Qasiyuni Kabara, from a prominent Qadiri family, resigned from the shari'a implementation committee in 1999 because it was so dominated by Salafis like Jafar Mahmud Adam.

214 100 **its first leader was Aminudeen Abubakar, an Islamic University of Medina alumnus:** Ibrahim Haruna Hassan, "An Introduction to Islamic Movements and Modes of Thought in Nigeria," Issue 1 of Working paper series (Institute for the Study of Islamic Thought in Africa), 2015, 27.

100 **imposes dress codes, busts bars and brothels, and adjudicates marital disputes:** Nigeria Stability and Reconciliation Programme, "Shari'a Implementation in Northern Nigeria Over 15 Years. Policy Brief No.2: The Case of Hisbah," October 2016. Accessible at: https://www.qeh.ox.ac.uk /sites/www.odid.ox.ac.uk/files /shari'a%20-%20POLICY%20 BRIEF%20TWO%20Final%20 Version.pdf. Accessed 1 June 2019.

100–01 **support for sharia remains high:** Brandon Kendhammer, "The Shari'a Controversy in Northern Nigeria and the Politics of Islamic Law in New and Uncertain Democracies." *Comparative Politics*, vol. 45, no. 3, 2013, 291–294.

101 **abducted 110 more girls from the town of Dapchi:** UNICEF, "More than 1,000 Children in Northeastern Nigeria Abducted by Boko Haram Since 2013," April 13, 2018. Accessible at: https://www .unicef.org/wca/press-releases /more-1000-children-northeastern -nigeria-abducted-boko-haram -2013. Accessed: 12 April 2019.

101 **were kidnapped from a girls' school in Zamfara state:** Nwafor, "Police Confirm Abduction of 5 Persons at Girls' School in Zamfara," *Vanguard,* 2 May 2019. Accessible at: https://www .vanguardngr.com/2019/05/police -confirm-abduction-of-5-persons -at-girls-school-in-zamfara/.

102 **Although he was from a humble background, he went to Medina with a scholarship to IUM:** Andrea Brigaglia, "A Contribution to the History of the Wahhabi Da'wa in West Africa: The Career and the Murder of Shaykh Ja'far Mahmoud Adam (Daura, ca. 1961/1962–Kano 2007)," *Islamic Africa*, Vol. 3 , No. 1, 2012, 3.

102 **who was on one of the regular Saudi recruiting trips to Nigeria:** Brigaglia, 5.

102 **he was recruited to preach at a new mosque in Maiduguri:** Author's interview with Andrea Brigaglia.

103 **there was an attempt to transfer the fiery Izala founder Ismail Idris to Borno:** Amara, "Shaykh Ismaila Idris," 77.

103 **the Ibn Taymiyya Center in Maiduguri:** Abdulbasit Kassim, Michael Nwankpa, and David Cook. *The Boko Haram Reader: From Nigerian Preachers to the Islamic State* (Oxford: Oxford University Press, 2018), 41.

103 **"This is our creed and method of proclamation":** *The Boko Haram Reader,* 27.

104 **pick up thousands of followers:** Omar Mahmoud, "Local, Global, or in Between? Boko Haram's Messaging, Strategy, Membership, and Support Networks" in *Boko Haram Beyond the Headlines,* Combating Terrorism Center at West Point, May 2018, 91. Accessible at: https://ctc.usma.edu/app/uploads/2018/05/Boko-Haram-Beyond-the-Headlines_Chapter-5.pdf. Accessed 15 May 2019.

105 **Osama bin Laden reportedly sent an aide to Nigeria with $3 million:** Benjamin, *Kingdom of the Unjust,* 112.

105 **holding a rifle that he periodically shot off:** *The Boko Haram Reader,* 355.

106 **By the 1990s, there were at least one hundred Saudi alumni in northern Nigeria:** Umar, "Education and Islamic Trends in Northern Nigeria: 1970s–1990s," 137.

108 **Yusuf's preaching was institutionalized by the Salafi clerical establishment based in Kano:** Abdulbasit Kassim, "Shaykh Aminu Daurawa, Boko Haram and the Theological Discourse on Suicide Bombing," 2017. Accessible at: https://medium.com/@ak61/shaykh-aminu-daurawa-boko-haram-and-the-theological-discourse-of-suicide-bombing-a8e5941c5035. Accessed on June 3, 2019.

108 **a "level of destruction unseen since the country's civil war in the late 1960s":** Hilary Matfess, "Boko Haram: History and Context," *Oxford Research Encyclopedia of African History,* October 2017. Accessible at: https://oxfordre.com/africanhistory/view/10.1093/acrefore/9780190277734.001.0001/acrefore-9780190277734-e-119. Accessed on June 5, 2019.

109 **Kano, like many northern states, has an extremely high divorce rate:** Rohana Yusof and Amina Lawal Mashi, "An Assessment of 'Zawarawa' Mass Marriage Programme in Kano State, Nigeria," *International Journal of Social Science and Humanity,* Vol. 5, No. 10, October 2015, 853.

110 **"progressive desire to care for the vulnerable and the Salafi desire to prevent extramarital sex":** Alexander Thurston, *Salafism in Nigeria: Islam, Preaching, and Politics* (Cambridge: Cambridge University Press, 2016), 236.

111 **he suspected that Daurawa had been sidelined because he was too personally charismatic:** Author's interview with Governor Abdullahi Ganduje's spokesperson, Aminu Yasar.

216   112   **the evolution of the mass
wedding perfectly shows how a
Salafi project was mainstreamed
by the government in Kano:**
There were about a dozen low-level
female Hisbah officers present
from villages in Kano, but they had
been given only twenty-four hours'
notice and the central Hisbah board
had not been informed or involved.
They mainly corralled and attended
to the hundreds of brides on that
very hot day.

113   **The main Saudi embassy
in Abuja distributes Qurans
printed in the King Fahd Complex
in Medina:** "We'll Promote Ebira
Qur'anic Translation, as One of
African Languages—Saudi Amb.,"
Greenbarge Reporters, May 4, 2019.
Accessible at https://www
.greenbreporters.com/featured
/well-promote-ebira-quranic
-translation-as-one-of-african
-languages-saudi-amb.html.
Accessed on June 3, 2019.

113   **Nigeria was second only to
Sudan:** 2016–17 dawa ministry
report.

CHAPTER FIVE

117   **IMN started as a campus
movement in the 1970s at
Ahmadu Bello University in
Zaria:** "A History of Shi'a and its
Development in Nigeria: The Case-
Study of Kano," Sani Yakubu Adam,
Journal for Islamic Studies, Vol. 36,
2017, 234.

118   **seventy-nine members had
been "martyred" by police and the
military:** Umar, "Education and
Islamic Trends in Northern Nigeria:
1970s–1990s," 141.

118   **the Nigerian military killed
at least 348 IMN followers,
including three of Zakzaky's sons:**
Amnesty International, "Nigeria:
Military Cover-up of Mass
Slaughter at Zaria Exposed," April
22, 2016. Accessible at https://
www.amnesty.org/en/latest/news
/2016/04/nigeria-military-cover
-up-of-mass-slaughter-at-zaria
-exposed/. Accessed May 19, 2019.

120   **The Constitutional Court
ordered his release in early 2016:**
Katrin Gänsler, "Nigeria: Tensions
Persist After Zaria Mass Killings,"
Deutsche Welle, December 14,
2016. Accessible at: https://www
.dw.com/en/nigeria-tensions
-persist-after-zaria-mass
-killings/a-36762231. Accessed
June 2, 2019.

121   **The Zakzaky affair has raised
solidarity protests across the Shia
world:** Ashish Tripathi, "Shi'as in
Lucknow want Indian Government
to Intervene in Nigerian Crisis," *The
Times of India* (December 20, 2015).

122   **it funneled money to the
Salafi-oriented Muslim Students
Society:** Hunwick, "An African
Case Study of Political Islam," 152.

122   **a debate that is still sold in
markets today:** Brigaglia, 9.

123   Iran, the UAE, Egypt, Kuwait, Bahrain, Yemen, and 'a lot of countries around the world': "Crown Prince Mohammed bin Salman Talks to TIME About the Middle East, Saudi Arabia's Plans and President Trump," *Time* (April 5, 2018). Available at https://time.com/5228006 /mohammed-bin-salman -interview-transcript-full/.

124   The first Sabuwar Gandu mosque: Isa and Wada.

124   the Emir of Kano decided to appoint a Sufi judge: Author's interview with Aliyu Yusuf Kakaki, a journalist in Kano and a nondenominational congregant at both mosques who helped facilitate the dialogue between them.

124   more than five hundred Salafi protesters, some armed with knives and machetes: Author's interview with Aliyu Yusuf Kakaki.

124   there was an anti-Salafi conspiracy at the highest levels of Kano government: Thurston, 140.

124   a Sufi businessman named Isa Karabiyu donated another piece of land: Author's interview with Aliyu Yusuf Kakaki.

126–27   where he cheerily dispenses religious advice: His questions, he told me at his home in March 2019, include whether it's okay to wear a soccer jersey with a

beer logo on it. His verdict was that it is allowed if you cannot easily find an alternative shirt.

127   On Facebook, he refutes Salafis based on their own texts: Thurston, 160.

127   even the Prophet Muhammad would respect the Tijani Shaykh Ibrahim Niasse if he came back to Earth: Author's interview with Badaruddin Garwa, registrar of the Rijiyar Lemo courthouse in Kano, where the Inyass case was initially adjudicated.

127–28   he eventually had to be released because it was impossible to give him a free and fair trial: Author's interview with Badaruddin Garwa.

128   he was honored as a martyr in the Friday prayer of the Grand Mosque of Mecca: Brigaglia, 3.

CHAPTER SIX

131   Its recruitment rate was more than eight times as high as France: Adrian Shtuni, "Ethnic Albanian Foreign Fighters in Iraq and Syria," *CTC Sentinel*, Volume 8, Issue 4 (April 2015), 12. Accessible at https://ctc.usma.edu/ethnic -albanian-foreign-fighters-in -iraq-and-syria/. Accessed on May 4, 2019.

132   The Kosovo War lasted for fifteen months: Tim Judah, *Kosovo:*

218   *What Everyone Needs to Know*
(Oxford: Oxford University Press,
2008), 2.

**135   Serb forces had already set
fire to the wood portico:** Sabri
Bajgora, *Destruction of Islamic
Heritage in the Kosovo War, 1998–
1999*, ed. Robert Elsie and Petrit
Selimi, Ministry of Foreign Affairs
of the Republic of Kosovo, 2014.

**135   the Saudis abruptly pulled
out of the project:** Schwartz, 191.

**136   Saudi Arabia was one
of the first countries to offer
humanitarian aid to Kosovo:**
Delinda Hanley, "Muslim Countries
Send Huge Shipments of Aid to
Kosovo Refugees," *Washington
Report on Middle East Affairs*, July/
August 1999. Accessible at: https://
www.wrmea.org/1999-july-august
/muslim-countries-send-huge
-shipments-of-aid-to-kosovo
-refugees.html. Accessed July 1,
2019. The article quotes the Saudi
chargé d'affaires in Albania, Saleh
Abdul Latif Santithini.

**136–37   so there is considerable
exchange of people and ideas
between the two countries:**
It is, however, a somewhat
recent phenomenon because
when Albania was ruled by the
extremely closed dictatorship
of Enver Hoxha, there was
little cross-border interaction
between Albanians in Albania
and Albanians in Kosovo and
Macedonia. That changed when
Albanian communism collapsed
in 1990.

**137   at the behest of Kosovo's
grand mufti, Rexhep Boja:** Khan, 96

**137   set up the Saudi Joint Relief
Committee (SJRC) for Kosovo and
Chechnya:** The Committee was
originally dedicated to Kosovo but
was merged with the coterminous
relief effort in Chechnya to
consolidate personnel and
resources inside the kingdom.

**137   It was the umbrella
organization for charities:**
Testimony of Evan F. Kohlmann
Before the Senate Committee
on the Judiciary, Subcommittee
on Crime and Drugs "Evaluating
The Justice Against Sponsors
of Terrorism Act, S. 2930," The
Role of Saudi Arabian State-
Sponsored Charitable Fronts in
Providing Material Support to
Foreign Paramilitary and Terrorist
Organizations (July 14, 2010), 8.
The Kosovo Interior Ministry's
database of foreign charities
indicates that Al-Haramayn
Islamic Foundation registered
on February 25, 2000; the SJRC
registered on April 25, 2000 while
WAMY registered on June 4, 2000.
None has a license to operate there
anymore.

**137   By the time NATO troops
were:** King Fahd bin Abdul Aziz, "A
Report on Saudi Relief for Kosovo,"
June 13, 1999. Saudi Press Agency.
Available online at: http://www

.kingfahdbinabdulaziz.com/main
/y0370.htm.

137 **Saudi aid was a mixed
bag of supplies and religious
paraphernalia:** Schwartz, 190;
Shpend Kursani, "Report Inquiring
into the Causes and Consequences
of Kosovo Citizens' Involvement
as Foreign Fighters in Syria and
Iraq," Kosovar Center for Security
Studies (2015), 86.

137 **which included funding 388
missionaries:** Schwartz, 191.

138 **supported more than thirty
specialized Quranic schools
in Kosovo's rural areas:** Isa
Blumi, "Political Islam Among
the Albanians: Are the Taliban
Coming to the Balkans?" Kosovar
Institute for Policy Research and
Development (2005), 9.

138 **a former member of the
Afghan mujahideen and a close
associate of Osama bin Laden:**
Testimony of Evan F. Kohlmann
Before the Senate Committee on
the Judiciary, 9.

138 **Western charities and the
Saudi committees regarded each
other with mutual paranoia:**
Testimony of Evan F. Kohlmann
Before the Senate Committee on
the Judiciary, 10.

138 **"But people react strangely
to Saudi Arabians":** Reuters,
"Fearing an Attack, NATO Raids
House That Saudis Just Left,"

April 3, 2000. Accessible at:
https://www.deseretnews.com
/article/752815/Fearing-an-attack
-NATO-raids-house-that-Saudis
-just-left.html. Accessed on July
7, 2019.

138 **personally chaired by then-
Prince, now-King, Salman bin
Abdul Aziz:** Gold, 144.

139 **funding kindergartens,
schools, orphanages, Islamic
centers, and mosques:** Harun
Karčić, "Islamic Revival in
Post-Socialist Bosnia and
Herzegovina: International Actors
and Activities," *Journal of Muslim
Minority Affairs*: 30 (4) (2010),
525–526.

139 **The Saudi High Commission
for Relief:** Karčić, 526.

139 **just as the Afghan conflict
was morphing into a civil war, the
Bosnian conflict flared:** Jonathan
Benthall and Jérôme Jourdan, *The
Charitable Crescent: Politics of Aid
in the Muslim World* (London: I. B.
Tauris, 2003), 129.

139 **joined the Muslim Bosniaks
as foreign fighters:** Benthall and
Jourdan, 135.

139 **which included Nasir Ahmad
Nasir Abdallah al-Bahri:** William
Racimora, Salafist/Wahhabite
Financial Support to Educational,
Social, and Religious Institutions,
European Parliament's Committee
on Foreign Affairs (June 2013), 12.

220   Accessible at http://www.europarl
.europa.eu/RegData/etudes/etudes
/join/2013/457136/EXPO-AFET
_ET(2013)457136_EN.pdf.

139   **Osama Bin Laden's
former personal bodyguard:**
Interestingly, the effort to bring
foreign *mujahideen* to join the
Kosovo Liberation Army was not
very successful. There were only
about twenty foreign fighters,
according to KLA commander
Ramush Haradinah, and most were
from other European countries
(Schwartz, 192). Partly this was
because NATO responded so
promptly in this conflict that
Muslim countries did not have to
raise a call to arms like they did in
the early stages of the Bosnian War.

139   **sent missionaries, books
and Qurans, and so forth to
postwar Bosnia:** Michael B. Bishku,
"Bosnia and the Middle East:
Current Political, Economic and
Cultural Ties," *Journal of Muslim
Minority Affairs,* 36:2 (2016), 211.

139   **a NATO raid into the Saudi
High Commission office in
Sarajevo turned up terrorist maps:**
Gold, 146.

140   **Saudi charities perfected
the combination of *igatha* and
dawa, relief and proselytization:**
Burr and Collins, 139.

140   **which forcibly dismantled
the foreign mujahideen unit in
1994:** Kepel, 251.

140   **The IIRO charity, in
particular, helped Afghan
veterans pivot to the Balkans:**
Burr and Collins, 144–145.

140   **helped other former
mujahideen get jobs with
charities, orphanages, and clinics
there:** Burr and Collins, 36.

140   **Al-Haramain also opened an
office in Tirana:** Gold, 144.

141   **Albanian-Ottoman governor
of Egypt, Muhammad Ali, crushed
a Wahhabi uprising there in the
1840s:** Blumi, 21.

141   **later angered the stodgy
Saudi clerical establishment and
was forced to decamp:** Andrew
Hammond, 152.

141   **which had little patience for
religion in general:** Meanwhile
in neighboring Albania, religious
life was put in a chokehold under
the world's first atheist republic,
declared in 1967 by the dictator
Enver Hoxha, so it's unsurprising
that Gulf charity almost
singlehandedly revived Muslim
life there too.

141   **Even in the Yugoslav era,
Saudi charities donated some
funds:** Marko Rakic and Dragisa
Jurisic, "Wahhabism as a Militant
Form of Islam on Europe's
Doorstep," *Studies in Conflict and
Terrorism* 35 (2012): 650.

141   **Serbs used minarets as
target practice and targeted Sufi
leaders for murder:** Bajgora, 7.

142   **a vast gray pyramidal complex with spikes running down the center like a spinal cord:** Author's confidential interview with Dukajgin Krasniqi of the Kosovo police.

142   **the country's top cleric visited Prince Alwaleed bin Talal in Riyadh:** "Prince Alwaleed receives president of Islamic Union & Mufti of Kosovo," *Arab News*, March 20, 2009. Accessible at: http://www.arabnews.com/node /322701. Accessed on 9 June 2019.

142   **on the superiority of Arab culture and the need to emulate the behavior of the first Muslims:** Blumi, 12–13.

142   **Skender Beg:** Blumi, 12–13.

143   **the SJRC provided "food, jobs, and hope," whereas Western aid agencies did not:** Blumi, 13.

144   **The SJRC distributed Salafi books through three branch offices:** Author's interview with Zuhdi Hajzeri.

144   **built ninety-eight primary and secondary schools in rural Kosovo after the war:** Shtuni, 11.

144   **The most promising students were enrolled in thirty Quranic schools:** Blumi, 15.

144   **a hundred unlicensed mosques were built:** Besiana Xharra, "Kosovo Turns a Blind Eye Towards Illegal Mosques," *Balkan Insight*, January 12, 2012. Accessible at balkaninsight.com/2012/01/12 /kosovo-turns-blind-eye-to -illegal-mosques/. Accessed on June 9, 2019.

144   **The construction of mosques remains poorly supervised:** Ibid.

144–45   **The Al-Haramain Islamic Foundation (AHIF), whose branches around the world were raided after 9/11:** "Al Haramayn's Millions in Kosovo," Zëri, October 2, 2014. Accessible at https://zeri .info/ekonomia/489/milionat-e-al -Haramayn-ne-kosove-foto/. Accessed on June 8, 2019.

145   **the Pristina office of AHIF destroyed most of its documents:** Secretary of State, "Terrorist Financing—Updated Nonpaper on Al Haramayn," Wikileaks Cable: 03STATE23994_a, dated January 2008, 2003, https://wikileaks.org /plusd/cables/03STATE23994_a .html.

145   **Al-Haramain also changed its name in Kosovo "at least ten times":** Author's confidential interview with Dukagjin Krasniqi of the Kosovo Police.

145   **Al Waqf Al Islami:** "Al Waqf-Al Islami in the Balkans," Radical Islam Monitor in Southeast Europe, January 24, 2014. Accessible at: http://www.rimse.gr/2014/01 /al-waqf-al-islami-in-balkans. html. Accessed on June 8, 2019.

222   **145   its branch in Kosovo still received regular requests from the president of the Islamic community of Kosovo:** Artan M. Haraqija and Visar Duriqi, "Study says Kosova Islamic Community Funded by Group Linked to Terrorism," *Koha Ditore*, August 17, 2012. Accessible at: http://www.islamicpluralism.org/2095/study-says-kosovo-islamic-community-funded-by.

146   The Kosovo branch of Al Waqf Al Islami was finally closed in August 2018: "Announcement of Suspension of NGO Activities 2018" [Memo], Republic of Kosovo, August 20, 2018. Accessible at https://map.rks-gov.net/desk/inc/media/07785AC8-B1B3-47F3-A3D1-C51957827EAF.pdf. Accessed on June 5, 2019.

146   The main headquarters of the charity has since been rebranded: https://alabraar.nl / and https://drimble.nl/bedrijf/eindhoven/k72289171/stichting-alabraar.html.

146   the Kuwait-based Revival of Islamic Heritage Society: Interior Ministry of Kosovo, "Foreign NGO Database" (2019), provided to author upon request.

146   The SJRC was very ambitious, at first: Schwartz, 194.

146–47   Bosnian authorities seized a number of files related to Osama bin Laden: Gold, 146.

148   once led an Islamic fighters unit in the KLA called "Abu Bekir Sidik": Deliso, 66.

149   "betrayed their improper knowledge of true Islam": Blumi, 15.

CHAPTER SEVEN

153   IUM became strained: Commins, 106.

155   a considerable fraction of students who study in immersive Wahhabi environments end up rejecting the approach: Michael Farquhar, *Circuits of Faith: Migration, Education, and the Wahhabi Mission* (Stanford, CA: Stanford University Press, 2016), 164.

156   This concept is typically used to brand non-Salafis as unbelievers or polytheists: Maher, 207.

157   Peja was one of the places most damaged by the Kosovo War: Bajgora, 17.

159   a cache of ISIS registration documents, dubbed "*mujaheed* data," leaked from Raqqa: Valerie Hopkins and Vincent Triest, "Exclusive: Kosovo's ISIS recruits," *Prishtina Insight* (March 14, 2016). Accessible at: https://prishtinainsight.com/exclusive-kosovos-isis-recruits/. Accessed on June 3, 2019.

159   preferred "obedient" recruits to highly educated, religiously convicted ones: Kursani, 69.

160   the fighters recorded in the mujaheed data: Also, while Kosovars remain largely pro-America, pro-EU, and pro-NATO but are hamstrung by a visa policy that does not let them easily visit most countries in Europe. Turkey, meanwhile, has visa-free entry for Kosovars.

160   Three-quarters of them were young people: Adrian Shtuni, "Dynamics of Radicalization and Violent Extremism in Kosovo," United States Institute of Peace (December 2016): 1. Accessible at https://www.usip.org/sites /default/files/SR397-Dynamics -of-Radicalization-and-Violent -Extremism-in-Kosovo.pdf.

161   there was no measurable correlation between poverty or unemployment and going to Syria: Shtuni, 7.

161   At least one Kosovar foreign fighter, Valon Musliu, studied in Saudi Arabia: Ayya Harraz, "Who Are the Kosovar Fighters in Syria?" Al Jazeera (February 11, 2016). Accessible at https://www.aljazeera .com/indepth/features/2016/02 /kosovar-fighters-syria-isil-iraq -kosovo-160211060736871.html. Accessed on June 9, 2016.

161   Eight of the eleven imams in Kosovo arrested between August and September 2014: Shtuni, 12.

161   was arrested in 2014 in Tirana on charges of recruiting "dozens" of fighters to Syria: Shtuni, 12.

161–62   "an extensive network of like-minded militants, supporters, and enablers": Shtuni, 2.

162   Enis Rama, a prominent Saudi-educated imam in Mitrovica, was arrested in September 2014: Kursani, 41.

162   another prominent Salafi imam, denounced Lavdrim Muhaxeri by name: "Shefqet Krasniqi: Lavdrim Muhaxheri Is the Heir to Hell." Gazeta Express (August 12, 2014). Accessible at: https://www.gazetaexpress.com /lajme-shefqet-krasniqi-lavdrim -muhaxheri-eshte-argat-i-dreqit -35789/. Accessed on June 12, 2019.

162   "They tell you something one day, something else another day, this and that, and they are cowards": Shpend Kursani, "Policy brief—Kosovo," Western Balkans Extremism Research and Policy Analysis Forum, British Council (August 6, 2018), 30. Accessible at: https://kosovo.britishcouncil.org /en/programmes/education-society /western-balkans-extremism -research-forum. Accessed on June 9, 2019.

162   At least one jihadist professed that he had been de-radicalized: Kursani, "Report Inquiring into the Causes and

224 Consequences of Kosovo Citizens' Involvement as Foreign Fighters in Syria and Iraq," 85.

162 **One young man in Pristina decided to become a more pious Muslim in his twenties and went to the nearest mosque:** Kursani, "Report Inquiring into the Causes and Consequences of Kosovo Citizens' Involvement as Foreign Fighters in Syria and Iraq," 77.

163 **There were even dormitories for young Salafi-jihadists in downtown Pristina:** Kursani, "Report Inquiring into the Causes and Consequences of Kosovo Citizens' Involvement as Foreign Fighters in Syria and Iraq," 80.

163 **Muhaxeri himself was a highly modern kind of jihadist:** Kursani, "Report Inquiring into the Causes and Consequences of Kosovo Citizens' Involvement as Foreign Fighters in Syria and Iraq," 84.

163 **The Salafi corpus seeded over the last two decades was ripe for rediscovery:** Behar Sadriu, "Grasping the Syrian War, a View from Albanians in the Balkans," *Nationalities Papers*, 45:4, 553.

164 **Four municipalities of Kosovo near the Macedonian border were disproportionately represented:** Shtuni, 1.

164 **also became something of a Salafi stronghold:** Macedonian Wahhabis have often come into violent conflict with the country's official Islamic community: In 2015, one Wahhabi imam, Ibrahim Shabani, tried to mobilize an armed group of fifty followers to capture IRC headquarters in Skopje. Saudi charities helped Macedonia after its war and there were even some Saudi fighters in the two foreign mujahideen units who aided the Macedonian Liberation Army, per a leaked Interior Ministry report.

164 **Salafi-jihadists maintained a cross-border jihadi recruitment camp:** Marko Babić, "Muslims and Islamic Fundamentalism in Macedonia." *Politeja* No. 30, (2014), 394.

164 **One ISIS recruit who did not end up going to Syria attended sermons organized by a charity in Kaçanik called Islamic Youth:** Frud Bezhan, "Inside Kosovo's Islamist Cauldron," *Radio Free Europe* (June 2016). Accessible at: https://www.rferl .org/a/inside-kosovos-islamic -cauldron/27825148.html. Accessed on May 30, 2019.

164 **Elez Han's foreign fighter rate was five times as high as that of the Belgian suburb of Molenbeek:** Shtuni 2016: 4.

166 **their sons had become Salafi Muslims or jihadists:** Kursani, "Policy brief—Kosovo," 32.

167 **the Kosovo police claim to have prevented four planned**

domestic terror attacks: Author's interview with Skender Preteshi.

171 **Afdiu's NGO, called Gjurma, which translated several Salafi texts into Albanian:** "Announcement of Suspension of NGO Activities 2018" [Memo], Republic of Kosovo, August 20, 2018. Accessible at https://map .rks-gov.net/desk/inc/media /07785AC8-B1B3-47F3-A3D1 -C51957827EAF.pdf. Accessed on June 5, 2019.

172 **Peace TV is an international Salafi channel founded by the radical Indian televangelist Zakir Naik:** "Zakir Naik Granted Saudi Citizenship," *The Star Malaysia* (May 20, 2017). Accessible at https://www.thestar.com.my /news/nation/2017/05/20/zakir -naik-granted-saudi-citizenship/. Accessed on June 13, 2019.

172 **Peace TV used to have physical headquarters in the city's Sunny Hill neighborhood:** Author's interview with Liridon Llapasthrica, who has twice been a guest on Peace TV as a political analyst and humanitarian worker.

172 **It's headed by the Pristina-based Salafi imam Enis Rama:** Behar Sadriu, "Rhetorical Strategies of Kosovo's Imams In the Fight for 'Women's Rights,'" in *The Revival of Islam in the Balkans*, ed. Arolda Elbasani and Olivier Roy (London: Palgrave Macmillan, 2015), 193.

173 **Naik was also awarded the annual King Faisal International Prize for Service to Islam in 2015:** Ishaan Tharoor, "The Saudi King Gave a Prize to an Islamic Scholar Who Said 9/11 Was an Inside Job," *The Washington Post* (March 4, 2015). Accessible at: https:// www.washingtonpost.com/news /worldviews/wp/2015/03/04/the -saudi-king-gave-a-prize-to-an -islamic-scholar-who-says-911 -was-an-inside-job/. Accessed on June 21, 2019.

174 **a Deobandi charity run by an exiled Kosovar, Xhemajl Duka, was closed:** Irfan Al-Alawi, "Extremists Establish Foothold in the Balkans," The Gatestone Institute (September 24, 2012). Accessible at https:// www.gatestoneinstitute.org/3360 /kosovo-peace-tv. Accessed on July 5, 2019.

176 **Kuwait's Society of the Revival of Islamic Heritage (RIHS) also gave a 286,000-euro donation to a charity in Kosovo:** "Kuwait Grants Kosovo EUR 286,000 for Projects Dedicated to Orphans," Kuwait News Agency, January 24, 2014. Accessible at https://www.kuna.net.kw /ArticleDetails.aspx?id=2357424 &language=en. Accessed on May 15, 2019.

176 **signed a 1.5-million-euro deal with the UAE's Minister of Finance, Sheikh Hamdan bin Rashid Al Maktoum:** "H. H. Sheikh

226 Hamdan bin Rashid Al Maktoum Allocates $1.5 million for Building 8 Endowments in Kosovo," Sheikh Hamdan bin Rashid Al Maktoum Award for Medical Sciences (May 11, 2014). Available at http://www.hmaward.org.ae/mobile/news_details.php?id=1407.

177 Turkey is building Pristina's new central mosque: Maxim Edwards and Michael Colborne, "Turkey's Gift of a Mosque Sparks Fears of 'Neo-Ottomanism' in Kosovo," *The Guardian* (January 2, 2019). Accessible at https://www.theguardian.com/cities/2019/jan/02/turkey-is-kosovo-controversy-over-balkan-states-new-central-mosque. Accessed on July 1, 2019.

177 The Diyanet, Turkey's Supreme Religious Council, has an office in Kosovo: Karčić, 527.

177–78 the Diyanet has taken over the organization of all Balkan Muslims' hajj pilgrimage: Kerem Öktem, "New Islamic Actors After the Wahhabi Intermezzo: Turkey's Return to the Muslim Balkans," paper presented at the conference "After the Wahhabi Mirage: Islam, Politics and International Networks in the Balkans" at the European Studies Centre, University of Oxford (June 2010), 33.

178 There are more than 1,300 students from Kosovo studying in Turkey now with scholarships: "Study in Turkey," 2019, Accessible at: https://studyinturkey.info/home-countries-a-b/f-kosovo/. Accessed on July 15, 2019.

178 In the historic southern city of Prizren, there is a small NGO called the Quran Foundation: Una Hajdar, "Kosovo Police Raid NGOs Linked to Iran," *Balkan Insight* (June 25, 2015). Accessible at https://balkaninsight.com/2015/06/25/kosovo-raid-ngos-with-ties-to-iran/. Accessed on May 2, 2019.

CHAPTER EIGHT

181 The Committee for the Promotion of Virtue and the Prevention of Vice is no longer allowed to arrest people: Reuters, "Saudi Arabia names new labor minister, reshuffles religious and Shura councils," December 3, 2016. Available at: https://www.reuters.com/article/us-saudi-politics/saudi-arabia-names-new-labor-minister-reshuffles-religious-and-shura-councils-idUSKBN13R2HE.

182 MBS has indeed diminished the resources dedicated to religious institutions: Stéphane Lacroix, "Saudi Arabia and the Limits of Religious Reform," Cambridge Institute on Religion & International Studies (February 25, 2019), 3–4. Available at https://religionanddiplomacy.org.uk/wp-content/uploads/2019/02/TPNRD-Lacroix-Saudi-final.pdf.

183   **He speaks at conferences with panels like "Moderation in Islamic History and Jurisprudence Heritage":** "Muslim World League Launches Global Forum for Moderate Islam," *Arab News* (May 27, 2019). Available at http://www.arabnews.com /node/1502441/saudi-arabia.

183   **"religious bookstores in Riyadh are full of books advocating the exact opposite":** Lacroix, 3.

183   **Saleh al-Fawzan, a strident anti-Shia ideologue, remains in good favor with MBS:** Ola Salem and Abdullah Alaoudh, "Mohammed bin Salman's Fake Anti-Extremism Campaign," *Foreign Policy* (June 13, 2019). Available at https:// foreignpolicy.com/2019/06/13 /mohammed-bin-salmans-fake -anti-extremist-campaign/.

183–84   **Most of the clerics who have tried to think critically about Wahhabism itself:** Lacroix, 5.

184   **"Saudi Arabia was not qualified to lead such a centre in view of its official doctrine of Wahhabism which they said inspired the IS [Islamic State] ideology":** Adam Abu Bakar, "Putrajaya Shuts Down Saudi-backed Anti-terrorism Centre," *Free Malaysia Today* (August 6, 2018). Available at: https:// besacenter.org/perspectives -papers/saudi-religious -moderation/.

185   **It included structured debates with Islamic scholars:** House 2012: 197.

185   **"most professional, comprehensive and successful":** Hamed El-Said, "De-Radicalising Islamists: Programmes and Their Impact in Muslim Majority States," *Developments in Radicalisation and Political Violence.* London: The International Centre for the Study of Radicalisation and Political Violence (January 2012): 35. Available at: https://icsr.info/wp -content/uploads/2012/02/1328 200569ElSaidDeradicalisation1 .pdf.

185   **"the lack of suspicious transaction reports, in particular on suspected cases of terrorist financing, is a concern":** "Saudi Arabia's Measures to Fight Money Laundering and the Financing of Terrorism and Proliferation," Financial Action Task Force (September 2018), 4. Available at: http://www.fatf-gafi.org /publications/mutualevaluations /documents/mer-saudi-arabia -2018.html.

185   **cannot operate abroad except through the King Salman Humanitarian Aid and Relief Centre or the Saudi Red Crescent:** Martin Williams, "FactCheck Q&A:

228 Is Saudi Arabia Funding ISIS?"
Channel 4 (June 7, 2017). Available
at: https://www.channel4.com
/news/factcheck/factcheck-qa-is
-saudi-arabia-funding-isis.

186 **Dawa Ministry staff worked
to convert thousands of Chinese
workers:** "245 Chinese Convert to
Islam in Saudi Arabia—April 2012,"
YouTube (April 22, 2012). Available
at https://www.youtube.com/watch
?v=lHW9FdpiORk.

186 **it stands to affect the pool
of over eleven million migrant
workers who now live there:**
Mohammed Rasooldeen, "Saudi
Arabia Has 11 Million Foreign
Workers from More Than 100
Countries," *Arab News* (December 1,
2017). Available at: http://www
.arabnews.com/node/1201861
/saudi-arabia.

187 **One of its leaders was a
Filipino preacher and convert to
Islam:** Reuters, "A Saudi Institution
Helps Foreigners Convert to Islam,"
August 23, 2007. Available at
https://reuters.screenocean.com
/record/188400.

187 **Arabic Qurans distributed
overseas:** Kingdom of Saudi Arabia,
Ministry of Islamic Affairs, da'wah,
and Guidance, "Statistical Yearbook
for the Fiscal Year 1438/1439"
[Arabic], 2017, Available at https://
www.moia.gov.sa/Statistics/Pages
/Details.aspx?ID=9 and Kingdom
of Saudi Arabia, Ministry of Islamic
Affairs, da'wah, and Guidance,

"Statistical Yearbook for the Fiscal
Year 1434/1435" [Arabic], 2015,
Available at https://www.moia
.gov.sa/Statistics/Pages/Details
.aspx?ID=4.

187 **The kingdom is basically
a rentier state and owes a lot
to its citizens:** Steffen Hertog,
"Challenges to the Saudi
Distributional Sate in the Age of
Austerity" in *Salman's Legacy: The
Dilemmas of a New Era in Saudi
Arabia,* ed. Madawi Al-Rasheed
(London: Hurst, 2018), 73–74.

187 **the kingdom has been
going on the international debt
market to sustain spending:** F.
Gregory Gause, III, "Saudi Arabia,
the United States and the Anti-
Iran Front in the Middle East," The
Hoover Institution (June 19, 2018).
Available at https://www.hoover
.org/research/saudi-arabia-united
-states-and-anti-iran-front
-middle-east.

189 **the "unacceptably broad
definition of terrorism" it uses to
crack down on its own civilians:**
Human Rights Watch, "Saudi
Arabia: New Counterterrorism
Law Enables Abuse" (November 23,
2017). Available at https://www
.hrw.org/news/2017/11/23/saudi
-arabia-new-counterterrorism
-law-enables-abuse.

189 **"the nation that serves as
custodian of the two holiest sites
in the Islamic Faith":** The White
House, "President Trump's Speech

to the Arab Islamic American Summit" (May 21, 2017). Available at https://www.whitehouse.gov /briefings-statements/president -trumps-speech-arab-islamic -american-summit/.

191   Qatar, which has an intense regional rivalry with Saudi Arabia, patronizes the Muslim Brotherhood-style Islamists that Saudi Arabia despises: Peter Mandaville and Shadi Hamid, "The Rise of Islamic Soft Power: Religion and Foreign Policy in the Muslim World," *Foreign Affairs* (December 7, 2018). Available at: https:// www.foreignaffairs.com/articles /middle-east/2018-12-07/rise -islamic-soft-power.

191   When Salafi charities from Kuwait go to Syria today: Zoltan Pall, "Kuwaiti Salafism and its Growing Influence in the Levant," Carnegie Endowment for International Peace (2014), 16. Available at https:// carnegieendowment.org/files /kuwaiti_salafists.pdf.

191   "It's not between Iran and Saudi Arabia": Crown Prince Mohammed bin Salman Talks to TIME About the Middle East, Saudi Arabia's Plans and President Trump," *Time* (April 5, 2018). Available at https://time .com/5228006/mohammed-bin -salman-interview-transcript -full/.

192   There are now over forty Turkish embassies in Africa: Peter Kenyon, "Turkey Is Quietly Building Its Presence in Africa," *NPR* (March 8, 2018). Available at https://www.npr.org/sections /parallels/2018/03/08/590934127 /turkey-is-quietly-building-its -presence-in-africa.

192   Turkey's largest overseas military base is in Mogadishu, Somalia: Asya Akca, "Neo-Ottomanism: Turkey's foreign policy approach to Africa," Center for Strategic and International Studies (2019), 4. Available at https://www.csis.org/neo -ottomanism-turkeys-foreign -policy-approach-africa.

192   from another angle, it's a return to form: The Hejaz, which includes Mecca and Medina, was an Ottoman territory from 1517–1918; the Ottoman rulers clashed periodically with the first two Saudi-Wahhabi states.